THE YOGIC KITCHEN

JODY VASSALLO

Contents

What is a yogic kitchen?

Firstly, let me say loudly THIS IS NOT A DIET BOOK. I also hope that you get more from this book than the pleasure of cooking the 100 fabulous recipes in here because this book is not just about food, either! I called this book *The Yogic Kitchen* not because I am an experienced yoga instructor, but because my yoga practice sits alongside Ayurveda, its sister science. And just as yoga is not just about the asanas (postures), neither is Ayurveda only about food. Ayurveda has way more to offer you than handy hints on what to eat. So, what is a yogic kitchen and what is Ayurveda? You don't have to practise yoga to have a yogic kitchen, but the benefits of yoga practice are well documented. A yogic kitchen is simply one where the principles of Ayurveda inform your daily menu.

Ayurveda is the traditional Indian healing system that is over 5000 years old, so the information I am sharing with you in this book is tried and tested; it has been passed down through generations. Ayurveda predominantly uses food as medicine to help people maintain their health and increase their longevity. It is, admittedly, my interpretation of it, but I have tried to be as faithful as possible to the practice.

I use Ayurveda on a daily basis in my health coaching practice and as a therapeutic tool with my yoga students to give them a deeper understanding of their bodies, minds and natural tendencies.

Ayurveda means science of life: *ayur* – science, *veda* – of life. It teaches that eating well is the foundation of one's health and when we are not eating well, the body will show symptoms of illness and disease. By following the recommendations in this book it is my hope that you will gain a greater understanding of how to achieve more balance and harmony in your own life. That's what happened for me when I discovered Ayurveda and it is the reason I continue to share my passion for this ancient science of wellness with the world through my books but also through my retreats and workshops.

THE THREE DOSHAS

The healing system of Ayurveda is based on the principle that five elements – earth, fire, water, air and space – exist both within our bodies and in the world around us. The elements combine in our bodies to form one's constitution. These five elements, in varying degrees, comprise the three doshas (otherwise known as energetic forces of nature or functional principles) that describe one's unique constitution (or *prakruti* in Ayurveda). The three doshas are known as Vata, Pitta and Kapha. Each dosha describes certain characteristics based on the elements they contain. Vata represents predominantly the quality of air, Pitta represents fire and Kapha represents water. We are all made up of varying amounts of each element and each person has a unique combination – we all have a unique proportional mix of the doshas but one may dominate. Some people have more air, others more fire and others more earth.

These elements govern the way our body responds to certain foods and lifestyle choices, and like increases like and opposites balance in Ayurveda. So a person with lots of fire in their constitution will be more susceptible to illness in the heat (Pitta dosha), a person with more water will be vulnerable in cold, damp and humid conditions (Kapha dosha) and a person dominated by air is shaken in cooler windier months (Vata dosha). The more you learn about the qualities of the elements that make up the doshas, the more it will help you determine the foods and other life choices that are best for you for balancing your dosha and that will create calm in your constitution. The elements don't just exist in nature, they are also present in the food we eat. Some foods are more heating, some more watery, some more crisp, light and airy.

A person with a dominant Pitta (fire) dosha will thrive in the cooler months or achieve balance in the hotter months by eating cooler foods. Whereas a watery person will celebrate the warm summer months and feel more energised while feeling challenged in cooler damper climes, and warm dry foods will provide relief for these people who can feel slow and sluggish. Airy types have an aversion to the cold and hide out from the wind, they need sunshine to warm their bones and nourishing cooked foods to ground their energy. (For more on the doshas, see pages 18–21.)

When our constitutions become out of balance from the wrong kinds of food, movement, routine or environment, then our health can suffer. This is known in Ayurveda as an imbalance and, no matter what your dosha, Ayurveda will treat and deal with the imbalance first. (For more on imbalance, see Balancing the doshas, pages 22–41.)

Vata	Pitta	Kapha
Air	Fire	Water
Space	Water	Earth

So I hope you are starting to get the picture that Ayurveda is a way of living; a large part of it is food but lifestyle is also vitally important. This book is an introduction to an ancient way of living, a tool to give you more insight into your body and how it is affected by the world we live in and the choices we make.

MY AYURVEDIC JOURNEY

When I was introduced to Ayurveda through yoga, it resonated deeply with me because it asked me to look at the things I was doing and question whether they were working for me.

I thought what I was eating was healthy, I followed nutritional guidelines and ate the recommended foods but I never had cause to query the concept of a one size fits all nutrition model.

However, once I started to investigate Ayurveda and research the foods that were appropriate for me and my body type, it became pretty obvious to me they were different to what someone of a totally different body shape could tolerate.

When I looked a little deeper, as Ayurveda asks you to do, and examined myself closely, I saw that I was a bit of a controlling mess. I had been practising a style of yoga that followed a macrobiotic way of eating that was far too heating for me. I was anti sugar and my diet was full of intensely flavoured foods with lots of soy sauce, chilli, curries, miso soup and tomatoes.

The increased heat that this diet created in my body didn't impact so much on my health but it had a field day with my mind. I had become a self-centred, highly motivated, competitive, hard-working perfectionist who had very little sweetness in her diet or her life. I functioned on overdrive with a highly regimented exercise regime, a full diary and very little time for fun or relaxation. When anything went wrong I just tried harder, worked harder and berated myself for being a failure. Nothing was ever good enough for my insane standards and I was angry and miserable.

Anyway, long story short, after carrying on like this for about 10 years I worked myself into the ground, lost my business and had a breakdown. The fire had burnt out!

Yoga was the only thing I felt would get me back on track so I took the crumbled me back to my mat, but this time I chose a different style of yoga and the principles of Ayurveda formed the foundation of this new practice. Yin yoga is a gentle, relaxing form of yoga with more passive poses and a slower pace. On those rare occasions I could quieten my mind for a moment at yoga, I started to hear messages I had needed to hear for a very long time. As I listened, I learnt that perhaps sweet stuff wasn't all bad and that all of those intense flavours I demanded and proclaimed essential to add flavour to a meal were not as good for me as I'd believed them to be.

So I started digging, learning and experimenting with both my diet and my lifestyle.

HOW THE AYURVEDIC LIFESTYLE HELPED ME

My research revealed that I was basically a Pitta (one with a fiery constitution) who was totally out of balance. I was eating all the wrong foods and if I continued doing all of the things that I had been doing, then the misery would continue. Unfortunately, before my meltdown my need to look good in the world had overtaken my need to feel good – I'd allowed my fire to become a raging inferno.

As a Pitta, I realised if I wanted to feel better, I had to learn how to chill out, slow down and eat in a different way. I started with the food because for me that was the easiest and the hardest place to start. (For Vata types the challenge is to quieten the mind and manage their fear and anxiety. If digestive issues have started to surface, then these also need to be managed. Kapha types often have an ongoing issue with their weight and energy levels.)

I'd never really had a struggle with sugar; I'd always been more drawn to the salty, spicier, more intense flavours. So after many years of eating very little sugar, I started to add it back into my diet and I don't

mean through eating lollies and cakes (though I did tell the sheriff in me they are allowed sometimes), I mean through adding more ripe seasonal fruit into my diet, sweet vegetables and grains, sweet spices to my porridges and on birthdays I'd bake a cake.

To remedy my intensity and hyper vigilance and to cool my mind, I introduced a little bit of dairy, but I was really mindful of how I did this. Not all dairy is suitable for Pitta types and of course the dairy I loved didn't love me. I needed to ease up on the parmesan and salty feta and eat more soft fresh cheeses.

I began adding ghee to everything and slowly things started to change. I started to change and finally after many years I felt myself relaxing and softening and feeling open to sitting still. Prior to looking into Ayurveda, just the thought of sitting still made me anxious; every time I sat down and stopped my mind revved up. I'd spent my whole life trying to out run, out work, out educate the voices that lived in there that told me I needed to be more, achieve more, know more blah, blah, blah ...

It wasn't until I was courageous enough to look at my work addiction and my Pitta attachment to success and being seen that the big stuff started to shift for me. You see, Ayurveda is here to help us create balance in all areas of our life and I needed to start looking at the elements in my life that had been missing.

My biggest challenge was learning how to do nothing; it still is. It is hard for me to avoid filling up my days. All of this is still a work in progress and I try not to take it too seriously, as my natural tendency is to be very serious and to want to try to be the best at everything I touch. Ayurveda has taught me so much about myself and a lot of it has been hard to see. Ayurveda has also taught me a lot about people around me and at first I would use it as a tool to diagnose and psychoanalyse everyone. I suggest you don't do that! When I first discovered it, though, I have to admit I was pretty obsessed with trying to figure out what doshas my friends and family were and offering loads of unsolicited advice about things they could change to make their lives better – oh so Pitta! These days I try to mind my own business and only offer suggestions when asked. I must be maturing!

As I head towards the Pitta Vata stage of my life (as different times of life are also governed by the three main doshas, more about this shortly) they say I am meant to become more sensitive, creative, wiser, spiritual, forgetful, stiffer and drier. I can feel myself letting go of the need to be seen in the world that I held onto so tightly in my 20s, 30s and 40s when my fire was burning bright. And even though I am in some way grieving the fire diminishing in me, I do on a deeper level feel it is time to step aside and let those younger high-energy entrepreneurs have their time in the sun. I am also called to honour the cycles and rhythms of nature and remember that I am just another small part of it.

Today I have given up my mad exercise regime, thank goodness. I know now that too much exercise will aggravate the Vata that is now rising in me, so instead of running, boot camping and vinyasa-ing, I take long walks with my beloved dog, teach a much more balanced style of yoga, practise yin yoga and surf.

I manage the heat in my body with cooling foods, healthy lifestyle choices, calm people, relaxing environments and spending time in nature.

I want you to know, I am not a saint and I don't follow the Ayurvedic eating plan with rigidity. I do still eat foods that are listed in the foods to avoid column for Pittas and accept the consequences. (See Food Charts For Vata, Pitta, Kapha at the back of the book, pages 240–5.) I cherish winter where my Pitta is at its calmest. I have learnt to love relaxing and best of all I have learnt to listen. I know humbly and wholeheartedly now that I am not always right, but I still really love when I am. I can now accept the differences in others and not see them as weaknesses. I understand that when I am angry or overheated it is about me and not about others and what they have done to me. I see I have an amazing ability to transform things and create something from nothing, and that is the gift of my Pitta, but most of all I know that the things I love often are not the best things for me.

Ayurveda has taught me to respect that we are all individuals and what works for one won't necessarily work for another. We are all on a journey of self-discovery; some will move a little faster than others but it is essential we honour the other person's path. Life is here to teach us the lessons we need to learn. We must all remember to listen to the voice inside of us as it knows the truth about how we feel. Following how I feel inside has never been easy but it's the best compass I have found.

Enjoy the ride.

Yoga is the journey of the self through the self to the self.

–The Bhagavad Gita

Using this book

Ayurveda is a gentle way of living. It is not my intention to be preaching to you here. Take what resonates with you and leave what doesn't. As with any changes to your diet, you may want to consult your GP or health practitioner before you begin. I don't demand that what is written on these pages be followed with such vigour you drive everyone around you nuts. Life is big, it is organic and it ebbs and flows. We are not in control: we have a say and we can try our best but we need to remember that life is not an exam, we are here to enjoy it and feel good in it.

I know that there will be times when it is easy to move through your day with ease, prepare your meals, eat the recommended foods, say all the right things, go for a walk, drink a herbal tea and finish your day feeling just super. And then there will be other days when it's a total nightmare, you will wake up feeling crap, you will eat something indulgent for brekkie and it will just continue to get more pear shaped from there. And that's OK. Enjoy every mouthful, I say.

I want you to go slowly with this, go gently and remain flexible. I am introducing you to Ayurveda to improve your life, not add another stress. It's all about balance and moderation, so cliché but so true when it comes to wellness.

To get started, first you need to figure out which doshas form your constitution, and then take a look if you are in balance or out of balance, which is perhaps what brought you to this book. All of that's in the next section. You will learn about the various characteristics of each dosha, then how to balance your constitution, followed by a little about the Ayurvedic approach to health, including the perfect daily routine and which foods to embrace and which to avoid if you are feeling out of whack. Of course, the bulk of this book is recipes, so once you know which dosha you are predominantly and that it is in balance, you could simply skip to that section and eat from there, confident that you are doing yourself some good.

There are Vata recipes that feature warming foods for autumn and early winter or for Vata types who need to reduce cooling foods, followed by Pitta recipes to cool you down in summer, and finally Kapha recipes for late winter and spring that contain astringent foods to help dry up the season's colds. These recipes will help you harmonise your doshas and help you gain a feeling of balance.

For those of you who need to know more, the endmatter (pages 228–245) provides even more information in the form of pantry information, food charts and other useful references.

Okay, hope that's all clear. Let's get into it!

Which dosha are you?

READING YOUR CHART AND DISCOVERING YOUR DOSHA

On the following pages are two charts that will help you figure out the particular mix of doshas that comprise your constitution. You may discover that you have some of the characteristics of all three doshas; this is not uncommon. But you will probably have one dominant dosha (Vata, Pitta or Kapha), then another dosha that is slightly less obvious, and so you would be, say, Vata Pitta, Pitta Kapha or Vata Kapha.

For example, I am a Pitta Vata. I have far stronger Pitta tendencies than I do Vata so I focus on managing my Pitta, but I do have to be aware of my Vata when I travel and in autumn and early winter, the Vata season (more on this later). You may find you are a Pitta Kapha, for example, and so you would focus on balancing Pitta generally but also managing Kapha tendencies in the Kapha season of late winter and spring or if you have a cold or cough, and you may need to manage the Kapha if you find you are gaining some excess weight in later years.

Be sure to look at both the physical and emotional/psychological/lifestyle/environmental characteristics of each dosha. A person may be physically a Kapha type but emotionally a Vata; this person would then be considered a Kapha Vata.

Just watch the tendency to make sweeping statements and generalisations about your doshas: there are a lot of factors and elements at play here. And what may appear to be someone's dosha may be a big imbalance that is demanding their attention. The world outside of us and the world inside us are ever-changing and so are we.

WHAT DOES TRIDOSHIC MEAN?

If, when you fill out the charts, you find you have an even amount of characteristics from Vata, Pitta and Kapha, you are described as being Tridoshic. This means you have a fairly balanced constitution but will still need to be aware of each dosha in its season. Ayurveda recommends tridoshic people follow a Vata diet usually because Vata is the dosha that goes out of balance first and the other doshas then follow. To obtain a more accurate and individual dosha reading and diagnosis, you may wish to seek out a consultation with an Ayurvedic practitioner.

Dosha evaluation charts

Go through the charts and tick the boxes, then add up the ticks. The one you have the most ticks under is your dominant dosha, the next your secondary dosha.

Normally we would suggest completing a dosha chart twice: the first time to establish your constitution (prakruti) and the second time to establish any imbalance (vikruti). Understanding your constitution will give you valuable insight into your tendencies; knowing your tendencies will help you manage your health and go a long way in helping you to create a balanced life for yourself. Each of us is made up of varying amounts of Vata, Pitta and Kapha energy. Vata provides us with movement and expression, Pitta governs our metabolic action and Kapha builds our tissues.

The first time you go through the chart, think about your body shape, emotional responses and personality up to about 18 years of age. If you can discuss this with your parents, you will often find they are able to share some valuable information with you about your behaviour in your younger years and they may have a much clearer memory of your size and shape.

The second time you fill out the chart, approach it from how you are now. Watch out for changes in weight, mood etc. to your formative years. Be honest and present. This can be a very helpful tool if used properly and you cannot get it wrong, as we are just trying to establish where your body is not functioning as it should.

If you complete the chart twice and your prakruti and vikruti are the same, then this is a good thing as it shows that your body is in a state of balance. But remember, the body is always in a state of flux, sensitive to outside influences and always trying to communicate any imbalance to you.

In Ayurveda we treat the imbalance to bring the body back to a state of health. Regardless of your constitution, you can experience an imbalance in any of the doshas. Imbalance is created from the external environment: not just the weather but any outside influences – food, habits, home environment.

A good way of determining your prakruti is by thinking about the things about you that never change. Body shape can fluctuate and cause some confusion but things like your basic personality tend to stay the same throughout your life.

Experience is simply the name we give our mistakes.

–Oscar Wilde

	VATA	PITTA	KAPHA
FRAME	Thin build; unusually short or tall; thin as a child; light bones and obvious joints; has a hard time putting on weight	Medium build; athletic, well-proportioned frame, often thinner at the waist; can gain and lose weight easily	Thick build; heavy bone structure; plump or chunky as a child; gains weight easily and finds it challenging to lose weight
WEIGHT	Low	Moderate	Overweight
EYES	Small, dark, dull, dry, brown, sunken Eyes that move a lot	Medium-sized, sharp, penetrating, green, grey, amber-yellow Sensitive to light	Big, blue, calm
LIPS	Dry, cracked, black/brown tinge	Red, inflamed, yellowish	Smooth, oily, pale, whitish
NAILS + FINGERS	Dry, rough, brittle, break easily Delicate, small, longer fingers	Pink, soft, flexible Regular fingers, pink nails	Thick, strong, oily, shiny Wide angular fingers, wide nails
HAIR	Black, brown, knotted, thin, dry, kinky, brittle, wiry	Soft, oily, yellow, blonde, early grey, red, fine, light Can often go grey or bald earlier than on other people	Thick, oily, wavy, dark or light
TONGUE	Cracked, tremors	Pink, yellow	White
NOSE	Slight, crooked, uneven	Sharp pointed, red nose tip	Wide, button nose
TEETH AND GUMS	Big, protruded and crooked teeth; emaciated gums	Medium-sized, yellowish teeth; soft gums	Strong and white teeth; healthy pink gums
NECK	Thin, tall	Medium	Big, folded
CHEST	Flat, sunken	Medium	Expanded, round
COMPLEXION	Dark, tans easily	Fair, freckled, prone to sunburn	Pale, hardly tans

	VATA	PITTA	KAPHA
BELLY	Flat, thin, sunken	Medium	Big, potbellied
HIPS	Slender, thin	Medium	Heavy, big
SPEECH	Fast	Sharp and cutting	Slow, monotonous
JOINTS	Cold, cracking, dry	More prone to inflammation than other doshas but no other issues	Large, well lubricated
SKIN	Dry, rough, cool, dark, brown, black; chaps easily; tans easily	Soft, oily, hot, fair, reddish, yellowish; sunburns easily	Thick, oily, cool, pale, white; tans slowly but evenly
LOVE	Falls in and out of love easily	Intense, passionate love affairs	Long-term relationships full of affection and love
DECISION MAKING	Struggles to make a decision	Makes decisions quickly; determined	Slow, thinks things through
SLEEP	Poor, interrupted	Little but sound	Heavy, likes sleep
APPETITE	Variable; sometimes poor; can be really hungry but then find it hard to eat all of the food on their plate	Good, sometimes excessive; gets angry when hungry or misses a meal	Slow but steady; can feel full on a small amount of food
EATING PATTERNS	Likes to snack and nibble, can forget to eat	Attracted to high protein foods like chicken, fish, meat, eggs, beans	Loves white foods – milk, pasta, dairy, bread Attracted to fatty foods
DIGESTION	Sometimes good but when out of routine it suffers, becomes irregular; forms gas, bloating	Quick but when disturbed causes burning, indigestion or reflux	Good but slower than other doshas; sluggish; forms mucus
THIRST	Variable	Excessive, usually thirsty	Rarely thirsty
UNDER STRESS	Anxious and worried	Angry and aggressive	Withdrawn, reclusive

	VATA	PITTA	KAPHA
BOWEL MOVEMENTS	Dry, hard, small pebbles; constipated, irregular	Soft, oily, loose; can tend to diarrhoea from too much spicy or oily food	Thick, oily, heavy, slow
VOICE	Low volume, hoarse, cracking	Loud and sharp	Pleasant, harmonious, low
PULSE	Thready, feeble, moves like a snake	Moderate, jumps like a frog	Broad, slow, moves like a swan
ILLNESSES	Suffers nervous disorders, gut problems, sharp irregular pains	Gets fevers, inflammation, skin conditions, rashes, hives	Prone to excess fluid, mucus, water retention
BODY TEMPERATURE	Cool hands and feet, little perspiration	Good circulation, sweats during exercise	Cool body temperature, moderate perspiration
PERSPIRATION	Scant with little odour	Intense during physical activities and gets hot sharp smell	Constant moderate sweet smell
CLIMATE	Prefers warm climate, sunshine, humidity	Prefers cooler climates, likes well-ventilated spaces	Happy with most climates but can suffer in damp and humidity
PHYSICAL ACTIVITY	Very active, hyperactive, finds it hard to sit still, often tapping a foot or moving some part of the body; exercise calms the mind	Moderate, likes to exercise to maintain physical strength and fitness; exercise helps control emotions	Lethargic, sedentary; very good stamina once started, enjoys lazing around; exercise keeps weight down
MENTAL ACTIVITY	Always active; creative thinker, changes mind and mood easily	Moderate; likes to analyse things, very intense thinker, loves to learn	Takes time to learn but then retains information well after that
MEMORY	Quick to learn, quick to forget	Learns quickly	Slow to learn, never forgets
CONCENTRATION	Finds it difficult to concentrate	Intense	Methodical

	VATA	PITTA	KAPHA
ROUTINE	Dislikes routine, always chopping and changing, doing lots of different things, may find it hard to focus on one task	Enjoys organising and thrives on self-directed routine	Works well with routine but can get in a rut
TEMPERAMENT/ EMOTIONS	Fearful, insecure, unpredictable, flexible, anxious when stressed	Aggressive, determined, impatient; prone to anger, hate, jealousy, irritability	Calm, slow, greedy, attached, loyal
CONTROL OF EMOTIONS	Gets upset but forgets easily	Gets angry, can hold emotions in	Does not upset easily, tends to withdraw
OPINION	Changes moods and ideas, sensitive to others' opinion	Strongly opinionated, likes others to know how they feel about things	Changes opinion slowly, may take some convincing, can be stubborn; avoids difficult situations
SPENDING	Spends money quickly, doesn't remember what on; believes money is there to be spent	Spends on luxury items; considers money should be spent on special things that will impress others and advance you	Spends on food; good at saving money
RELATIONSHIPS	Moves from one group of friends to another, independent, insecure	Jealous, likes their own way, outgoing, assertive, leader	Possessive, gets very attached, good listener, follower, lots of friends
SEXUAL INTEREST	Variable, can live in a fantasy; believes in happy ever after	Strong sexual interest and drive	Steady sexual interest and drive; said to be the most fertile of the doshas
DREAMS	Fearful; flying, jumping, running; dreams regularly but often doesn't remember them	Fiery; anger, violence, war; remembers dreams easily, often dreams in colour	Watery; river, ocean, lake, swimming, romantic; usually only remembers dreams if they are intense or if they relate to a current situation
FAITH	Changeable	Fanatic; faith based upon knowledge	Steady; faith based upon love

The doshas

THE VATA INDIVIDUAL

Vatas are the skinny tall folks, who can struggle to put on weight no matter what they eat or how much they eat. Vata rules movement, creativity and communication in the body, so it is easy to see why Vata types find it hard to sit still, love a chat and may have wild imaginations. You may notice them chattering away to themselves or telling a long-winded story. Because they have so much going on inside their heads they find it difficult to listen, their eyes may dart about as you talk to them and they are very easily distracted. Vata types may be more fearful and anxious of everyday things than others and tend to be light sleepers. Sensitive Vata souls suffer without a routine to stabilise and ground the air and space in them.

Quick to learn but also quick to forget, they may be more interested in the arts and creative activities than reading, writing and arithmetic. Without a routine, they may appear scattered and a bit all over the shop. Vatas often find themselves surrounded by mess, which can be a direct reflection of their state of mind. Vatas tend to overthink everything and find it difficult to make decisions. Vatas suffer under stress. They make friends quickly and change friends often, and can have difficulty forming close relationships. This is also reflected in their interests. Intensely interested in one thing momentarily and then onto the next thing before you know it. The qualities of the dosha are light and mobile so this is natural behaviour for their constitution.

Vata types are incredibly soft and intuitive and are greatly affected by the moods of those around them; when things get overwhelming for them they may just drift off into their minds where things are more comfortable for them. They are insatiable daydreamers. Anxiety and constipation can be a symptom of Vata imbalance. It is important that these types stay warm, slow down and create a routine for themselves to help balance the air and space in their dosha.

The qualities of Vata are like the wind – quick, light, dry, cold, subtle, mobile and rough. Vatas will often have dry cracked skin, hair and lips. They feel the cold and will often complain of cold hands and feet. They love the sun and their holiday of choice will most likely be a beach destination. They are disturbed by the wind and excess travel. They are drawn to crispy, crunchy foods but these foods will quickly send them out of balance. They have joints that crack and their bodies are the most fragile and sensitive of the three doshas because of the dry, light qualities of their constitution. The mobile quality may allow them to be efficient multi-taskers but it is essential they get plenty of rest to help them deal with the constant movement as they are delicate types. Vata types may also have a tendency to swing drastically in terms of weight, and flip from being underweight to overweight quickly. Things are everchanging with Vata individuals, be it in their homelife, workplace, relationships or physical body.

Their subtle nature may mean they are drawn to the spiritual and they have a natural tendency to seek out more esoteric experiences than the other two doshas. Vata types are most comfortable in nature by a running stream, listening to birds and gazing up at the stars. Vatas can be shy, insecure and awkward in social situations and one of their biggest challenges is to come to a place of self-acceptance. This fast paced modern world is often confronting to these Vatas, who may worry and struggle to keep up and fit in.

For more information on Vata out of balance, see page 24.

THE PITTA INDIVIDUAL

Pitta types love to be the centre of attention. Ruled by the elements of fire and water, they are born to shine and it's hard to mistake when a Pitta enters a room. These types like to be in control and are easily annoyed if made to follow rules and regulations. Pitta children are happy to figure things out for themselves and like to receive praise and recognition when they are successful. Blessed with strong athletic bodies, Pittas are driven, competitive individuals who play to win. Anger is their go-to emotion and if they don't get what they want, they can make things uncomfortable for all around them.

Pittas are fiery types whose qualities are hot, oily, sharp, light, spreading and liquid. The oily nature gives Pitta types lovely moist soft skin, though it can overheat easily and Pittas will often sweat a lot in hotter weather or suffer from acne, a spreading rash or hives. In life, oiliness means Pittas are very good lubricators when it comes to getting what they want out of life and situations.

They will often use their sharp tongues to ensure you understand their point of view.

Because fire rules transformation and is adept at converting ideas into objects or experiences, Pitta types are great at creating, planning, organising and executing as long as they are the ones running the show. They are energetic, ambitious, aggressive and arrogant about their pursuits, and will often blaze their way down their chosen path with little consideration for those around them. Pittas' egos need to be kept in check and it is their life lesson to learn to control their self-imposed will and fiery mind and nature. Pitta types can have a tendency to 'burn out' if they do not learn to moderate their desires for material possessions. Pittas need to learn patience and to consider others to temper their fires. Pitta types are courageous and make great leaders, as their ability to see a project through to the end is unrivalled by the other doshas.

They have strong, hot digestive systems, a fast metabolism and enormous appetites, and can get very hangry (angry when hungry) if they miss a meal. They may have heat rising in the body if their digestive system is overloaded, complaining of heartburn, ulcers or reflux. Emotionally, it may show up as fiery outbursts, heated conversations or an angry silence. Drawn to intense flavours (chilli, salt, hot'n'spicy) in food and drinks, and intense conversations and experiences, these folks are bored easily and are always on the lookout for the next exciting adventure. Pittas need cooling environments, calm friends and gentle interactions to balance out their natural tendency to overheat, overachieve and overdo. As kids, they often complain they are bored. Pitta rules the eyes and vision, so to calm their forceful nature they will do well painting or surrounding themselves in nature's beauty. Pitta types care very much about looks. They can become obsessed with their physical body, clothes and like to be seen and acknowledged for their appearance; they like to be seen as ahead of trends, and fashion can become another way they seek attention. Anger, impatience, skin issues, overheating and reflux can be a symptom of Pitta imbalance. It is important that these types learn how to manage heat and ambition. Pitta types often go grey before other types and Pitta men tend to lose hair earlier than the other doshas. For more information on Pitta out of balance, see pages 28–9.

THE KAPHA INDIVIDUAL

Kaphas are caring, maternal, graceful, sensual types. They tend to be focused more on others than on themselves and they can usually be found mothering something or someone. It is said that without Kaphas there would be no home, no children and no family, as Kapha energy ensures the stability and foundation of the home. They have a larger rounder body shape than the other two doshas and tend to put on weight just by looking at food. Ruled by the elements of earth and water, they have a sluggish metabolism and a tendency towards fluid retention. Weight issues are a constant headache for these individuals. Kaphas have thick wavy lustrous hair that is usually blonde or black.

Slow to learn but then they never seem to forget, these people can often be mistaken for being slow or dumb, especially when they are younger. If their teachers don't have the time or patience to spend extra effort going over things with them, they quickly fall behind at school.

Kaphas are most happy in their own company or being with family. They won't go out of their way to make friends as they can find friendships exhausting as they always seem to be the ones giving.

Though ruled by earth and water, the qualities of Kapha are most like water – moist, slow, cool, heavy, dense, cloudy, unctuous, stable and viscous. They have soft well-lubricated joints and often their bodies feel cool, soft and slightly moist to touch. They feel the cold and tend to have an aversion to the cooler months. Their heaviness is evident in their body shape but is often more of an issue for these types mentally as it can give them a heavy outlook on life. They are also heavy sleepers who like to sleep for longer periods of time. Kaphas are slow walkers, talkers and thinkers, and won't be rushed into decisions about anything; Kaphas are always calculating their energy and whether the effort is worth the expenditure. They seem to have a stubborn aversion to change and will often get stuck in unhappy relationships or work situations for long periods.

They are good savers and like to accumulate wealth and have a stable bank balance as this provides them with a strong sense of security. Kaphas love routine and stability but this can work against them if they are in an unhealthy situation. Kaphas can be very attached to the material world; they have a tendency to ground themselves in the world through food, people and possessions. They can become hoarders if this is not kept in check. Their home is everything to them as this is the place they devote to nurturing their families and loved ones. Kaphas are providers and nurturers, and they love to indulge in things they love. Kapha mothers need to be very aware this doesn't turn into smothering their children as they age and want to move away from home. Kaphas can fall into the trap of loving home so much they isolate from the world, especially in the cooler, damper months. This can lead to them becoming lazy, lethargic and gaining weight.

Kaphas have strong, dense, stable bodies and Kapha types are said to be the most resilient of all the doshas when in balance. They have strong bones and when physically fit they develop strong muscles and great endurance, especially once they are committed to a task.

Exhaustion and depression can be a symptom of Kapha imbalance. It is important that these types rise early, between 6am–10am is Kapha time of day and when they feel most sluggish. If they don't move their body in the morning, they can easily spend the rest of the day feeling tired, sluggish and unmotivated. Under stress, Kaphas will oversleep, overeat and do their best to avoid addressing whatever is bothering them. For more information on Kapha out of balance, see pages 32–4.

See Balancing the doshas on pages 22–41 for the causes of an 'imbalance' and what can make someone dominated by particular doshas unwell, and recommendations on diet and lifestyle to help balance your dosha.

Be ground. Be crumbled so wildflowers will come up where you are. You've been stony for too many years. Try something different. Surrender.

–Rumi

Balancing the doshas

Balancing your dosha is pretty straightforward and if I could give you one bit of advice, then that would be to 'keep it simple'. It takes a little while to get to know the qualities of your dosha but once you have familiarised yourself with the main characteristics of your dosha you will find it becomes second nature to remove things from your environment that are aggravating you.

Knowing the elements that govern your dosha is essential. Vata is ruled by air and space, Pitta by fire and water and Kapha by earth and water. Overexposure to the elements that govern your dosha will send you out of balance.

The principles behind balancing the doshas are guided by the Ayurvedic approach to health (see pages 42–6) and circadian rhythms (see pages 47–63).

The recipes I have written for this book are all designed to balance your doshas and have been carefully designed to maintain that balance, particularly in the season that your dosha will be more vulnerable. For Vata types I have created warming nourishing meals with ingredients that help to calm and soothe the anxious energy in the body and to stimulate the digestive system. Pitta recipes are more cooling and wholesome, designed to satisfy the strong Pitta appetite and moderate heat in the body, particularly in the warmer months and climates. The Kapha recipes I have created are naturally a little lighter and purposed with spices and ingredients to absorb the excess moisture and weight that Kapha types hold in the body.

To help you to shop and make your food choices, refer to the food charts for Vata, Pitta and Kapha at the back of the book on pages 240–5. I still use these tables a lot even after all these years, especially if I'm Vata imbalanced, as the foods differ quite a bit to the Pitta foods I normally favour.

VATA

To summarise what we have discussed earlier, Vata individuals tend to have thin, light frames; they are quick thinkers and can be quite nervy and excitable.

The Vata dosha is responsible for communication, movement and elimination of all wastes from the body. Someone may be either Vata in their constitution or they may have a Vata imbalance. Vata imbalances are very common for people who reside in cities and have busy lives.

Air and space dominate this dosha and they also aggravate it. They are susceptible to the cold and wind so it is essential they keep warm, maintain a routine and nourish themselves with warm cooked foods; it is logical that elements that decrease and calm this dosha are earth, fire and water.

They are aggravated by bitter, pungent and astringent tastes, and calmed by sweet, sour and salty.

Elements

- Elements that dominate this dosha – Air and Space
- Elements that aggravate this dosha – Air and Space
- Elements that calm this dosha – Earth, Fire and Water
- Tastes that aggravate the dosha – bitter, pungent and astringent
- Tastes that calm and balance the dosha – sweet, sour and salty

Time of day

Each dosha has a time of day when it is more obvious in the body and mind. For Vatas it is 2am–6am and 2pm–6pm. Vata types may find themselves becoming more anxious or fearful at this time of day, they may also wake at night and not be able to fall back asleep, especially if they are worried about something.

Time of year

In autumn and early winter Vata can be more aggravated in the body. The wind at this time of year can aggravate Vata types and it is important that they stay warm and out of the wind if it bothers them. When it gets windy and cold, the time has come to slow down and eat grounding, nourishing meals. Flavours that calm in autumn are the sweet, salty and sour.

Vata types struggle at this time of year as they are naturally cold and sensitive to air and movement. The autumn wind can play havoc with their digestive system as well as their minds, leading to episodes of anxiety.

Time of life

70 to 75 years and above is the time that Vata will be more prominent in the body.

Vata is responsible for feelings of joy and happiness, as well as creativity, speech, sneezing, movement and elimination.

I will not let anyone walk through my mind with their dirty feet.

–Mahatma Gandhi

VATA OUT OF BALANCE

The site of Vata in the body is the nervous system, and it governs the mind, colon, skin, ears, blood flow and breath – and it is where Vata will present more strongly when it is out of balance.

Signs that Vata is out of balance

When Vata people's health goes out of balance, the symptoms usually appear first in the gut or the mind. They might complain of an upset tummy, gas, bloating, small pebbly stools that are dry, hard, dark brown and sink. They can easily become constipated or irregular, especially when travelling or away from home. They may strain when passing stools and can find it painful.

Anxiety, weight loss, restlessness, fatigue, insomnia, interrupted sleep or fearful dreams, hypertension, inability to concentrate, tremors or a nervous system disorder are all indications that Vata is out of balance. Other indicators are dry cracked skin and lips, arthritis and joint pain.

Vata types are more likely to go out of balance in autumn and early winter.

Autumn–early winter/Vata health issues: constipation, gas, bloating, anxiety, dry skin.

Habits and lifestyle factors that imbalance Vata

Eating too many cold icy foods and drinks, especially anything with bubbles, such as sparkling mineral water, carbonated drinks and foods that produce gas in the body; excess raw foods such as salads, especially in the colder months; irregular meals or skipping meals; too much travel; being outside in the cold and the wind; lack of sleep and routine; spending too much time in front of the computer and TV; stress, overthinking and over talking all imbalance the Vata dosha.

Environmental effects

Wind will unnerve them and you may notice their behaviour and mood change if exposed to too much of the air element, as they already have this as a major part of their constitution. Unsettled weather can have a strong effect on Vata types. Autumn can be difficult, accordingly.

Air travel can greatly disturb these types and they need to ensure they limit flying if they are feeling insecure, fearful and anxious. Their Vata body needs nurturing. Vatas have cold, dry skin that is very susceptible to the cold and wind. Daily warm sesame oil massage will benefit them greatly. It is essential they keep their bodies warm, both internally and externally. Fear and anxiety can really inhibit the lives of Vata types so it is essential they create a comfortable, safe, stable home for themselves.

KEY Warmth, safe calm environment and routine

AVOID Cold, dry, windy environments, skipping meals, raw food, chilled drinks, carbonated drinks, excess movement and air travel

HOW VATA MANIFESTS IN THE BODY

Cold – Coldness appears in the hands and feet. Vatas will have a tendency to avoid cold temperatures and love warmer climes. They have poor circulation and can suffer from cold bones and stiffness.

Dry – Dryness is a major issue for Vatas. They often have dry skin, hair, lips, tongue and a husky voice. Dryness in their colon usually leads to them suffering from constipation.

Light – Vata individuals are generally light in body weight with fine muscles and bones. They sleep lightly and wake easily, with little noise needed to disturb them.

Rough – Roughness appears in the body as cracked skin, nails, split ends, cracked lips, teeth and joints that creak and crack when moved.

Subtle – They will suffer from an underlying subtle anxiety, fear or insecurity. Vata types are prone to goose pimples, muscle twitches and tremors.

Mobile – Vatas can't sit still: they walk fast, talk fast and tend to be those people who are incredible at multi-tasking. They are good at making money and great at spending it. Their eyes will dart around the room as they talk to you with their hands or shake their leg or tap. They love to travel and find it difficult to stay in one place for too long. Their moods are ever changing, as are their faith and their thoughts. Vatas love change and do what they can to make it happen often.

Clear –This quality gives Vata their clairvoyant ability, as this is related to the element of space. They can understand easily but forget abruptly, and they often experience a deep sense of loneliness.

Astringent – They can suffer from a dry choking feeling in their throats, and they will often find themselves with hiccoughs or burping. They enjoy oily, sweet, sour and salty foods.

BALANCING VATA

Vatas need routine, warm fluids, rest, massage, steady nourishment, warmth, decreased stress, and they need to avoid skipping meals, eating on the run, fasting and alcohol.

Activities that will calm Vata

Gentle calming exercise such as yoga, quigung (qigong), dance, golf, walking, swimming, listening to calming music, gardening, pottery, cooking, massage, meditation and getting to bed early all help Vatas to settle.

Warming grounding remedies – walking barefoot on the grass, warm sesame oil massage, foot massage, gardening, warm milky drinks with cardamom and cinnamon, ghee added to food and drinks

Warming grounding lifestyle choices – gardening, yoga, guided meditation, creative pursuits, listening to calming music

Lifestyle factors to limit – constant change and movement, overexercise, excess meditation without proper supervision, too much time on devices such as computers, TV, phones

So-called healthy foods that may imbalance you – raw food diets, juices, chilled smoothies and smoothie bowls, sparkling mineral water

Emotions and diet

Vatas are often attracted to cold, dry, crisp foods but these are best avoided. They can easily become imbalanced if they eat too many of these foods. Too much bitter, pungent and astringent food can also have a negative impact on the digestive system of Vata. The skin and body can become very dry in the colder weather and so Vatas should introduce warming spices and increase the amount of protein they are eating.

Soups and slow cooked stews made with plenty of root vegetables are the perfect choice for Vata types in the cooler or more unsettled months, and they do really well to warm their meals with spices like cinnamon, clove, star anise, cardamom and ginger that will help stimulate their digestion. To calm themselves they need to increase the amount of naturally sweet, salty and sour foods they are consuming. A glass of sweet warm milk before bed is a perfect remedy for any Vata that has trouble sleeping.

Routine and exercise

Vatas need to allow plenty of time for stillness in their day. Moving is what comes naturally to Vatas so they will often want to exercise and be on the go when they are feeling fragile, anxious or emotional. This is not the healthiest option, especially at the Vata time of 2pm–6pm. Their fragile nature demands they don't allow too much space between meals. For continued wellness, Vatas should eat their meals at the same time every day. Skipping meals is one way to quickly imbalance these people. The digestive system is where Vata types are most susceptible and they may have issues with gas, bloating and constipation. They have sensitive tummies that do best with nourishing home-cooked meals.

Eating on the run or snacking instead of eating a proper meal is not a good idea for these types. If they do want to move their body, they are best to try grounding practices like yoga, tai chi or even a gentle walk. More strenuous types of exercise should be done between 6am and 10am in the morning at Kapha time.

Quiet time, listening to music, reflecting, drawing or journaling will help to calm them. Before bed they are better to read than be on their phone or computer, as any device will aggravate the Vata energy in the body.

We enter the Vata stage of our lives at around 75 years of age so it is not uncommon for these types to become more dreamy, vague or fragile as they age. The best diet for Vatas includes warming and soothing foods that are stabilising for a light, airy constitution. (See charts at the back of the book, pages 240–5.)

PITTA

Pitta individuals are dominated by the element of fire. This creates heat in the body and is responsible for metabolising, transforming, digesting and processing all of our thoughts and all we eat. Pitta is also in charge of maintaining our digestive fire (agni); if our digestive fire is low, we will have problems with digestion and suffer from heartburn, reflux and indigestion.

Pittas have quick, sharp minds and tongues, a moderate body frame and tend to be able to maintain their weight better than the other two doshas.

Elements

- Elements that dominate this dosha – Fire and Water
- Element that aggravates this dosha – Fire
- Elements that calm this dosha – Air, Water and Earth
- Tastes that aggravate the dosha – salty, sour, pungent
- Tastes that calm the dosha – sweet, bitter, astringent

Time of day
10am–2pm and 10pm–2am is the time of day when Pitta will be more obvious in the body and mind.

Time of year

In summer Pitta can be more aggravated in the body. It is the season when Pitta health issues such as eczema, heartburn, reflux, headaches, hay fever, insomnia or burnout can arise. Summer is known as Pitta time (bile). Energy and heat rise up in the body in summer so it is important to keep cool. We are naturally drawn to cooling summer fruits and higher carbohydrate grains like rice. We drink more juices made from seasonal fruits and fill up on salads with cooling herbs.

More fiery Pitta types need to eat with more awareness in this season, and so too does anyone who starts to show any signs of heat in the body, such as skin issues, headaches, reflux, indigestion or insomnia.

Time of life

18 to 50–55 years is the time that Pitta will be more prominent in the body.

Pitta is responsible for regulating body heat through the metabolism of food, appetite, energy production, vitality, ambition, confidence, courage, learning and understanding.

PITTA OUT OF BALANCE

The site of Pitta in the body is the eyes, skin, stomach, small intestine, sweat glands, blood, fat – where Pitta will present more strongly when it is out of balance.

Signs that Pitta is out of balance in the body

Irritability, impatience, anger and pushy, aggressive behaviour; skin irritations and rashes; heartburn, reflux and peptic ulcers; headaches, eye problems, falling hair, early greying, hot flushes; waking in the middle of the night and unable to get back to sleep; excess sweating, acne, blood shot eyes, heavy periods, large clots; extreme hunger before menstruation; yellow urine or loose unformed stools that fall apart in water, sink or float with a strong, pungent, offensive smell; a need to use the toilet 2–3 times a day, and may be urgent; tendency to diarrhoea and urinary tract infections.

Pitta types are more likely to go out of balance in summer.

Summer/Pitta health issues: Eczema, heartburn, reflux, headaches, hay fever, insomnia, burnout.

Habits and lifestyle factors that imbalance Pitta

Eating too many hot, spicy, pungent, salty or sour foods; excess meat in the diet; too much alcohol; overanalysing or overworking; overexposure to heat and sun; intense conversations, pushing oneself too hard, emotional trauma, holding emotions in; skipping meals or fasting; exercising outside in the sun in the middle of the day in summer; not rinsing off the saltwater after swimming at the beach in summer.

Environmental effects

Determined high achievers, Pittas do well to spend time in nature connecting with the earth. Winter is the time they will feel their best if they can allow themselves to slow down and enjoy the cooler weather.

KEY Moderation, rest between work, quiet calm atmosphere, meditation, coolness, nature's beauty

AVOID Skipping meals or overeating, artificial stimulants, too much sun and sauna

BALANCING PITTA

Heat can very easily send Pittas out of balance and although they are often drawn to hot, spicy flavours, they would do well to stay away from these flavours, especially in summer or when they are feeling angry and stressed. When out of balance, the fire rises up and out in the body and can show up as fever, impatience, ulcers, indigestion, skin rashes, headaches and reflux.

Pitta types are attracted to beautiful things and are very focused on making money and acquiring beautiful things. They are hard workers who need to learn how to relax and temper the fire within them before it overwhelms them.

Activities that will calm Pitta

Eating when you are hungry rather than when you are starving, gentle calming exercise, spending time in nature, being by the water, moonlight walks, yoga, dance, non-competitive sports, walking, swimming, gardening, writing, massage with coconut oil as it is cooling, meditation, expressing emotions, getting to bed before 10pm, staying cool, sipping cooling herbal teas.

Cooling remedies – rubbing coconut oil into the skin, chilled rose tea bags over the eyes, cooling the feet

Cooling lifestyle choices – music, meditation, yin yoga, spending time in nature out of the sun, resting by still water

So-called healthy foods that may overheat you – ferments, yoghurt, kimchi, kombucha, sauerkraut

Lifestyle factors to limit – running in the middle of the day, sunbaking, hot yoga, power yoga, holding in emotions, alcohol, out in the sun without a hat, smoking, saunas

HOW PITTA MANIFESTS IN THE BODY

Hot – Pittas have strong digestive fire which means they can usually eat a lot, and often, and they tend to get quite cross if they try to go without food when they are hungry. They tend to have a higher body temperature than other doshas and can become quite agitated in the heat.

Sharp –They can have pointed sharp teeth either side of their front teeth, and sharp piercing eyes. Their features are strong and distinct, and quite angular. Pittas' minds are quick and extremely sharp, and they are blessed with a strong memory, but their speech can be cutting. They tend to work in short sharp bursts and can become irritable if overworked. When they suffer from pain it is usually hot and piercing.

Light – Their frame is usually light/medium and, because Pitta rules the eyes, they can also suffer from an intolerance to bright lights. Their skin is light and lustrous.

Liquid – The liquid attribute is demonstrated in the waste products, loose light oily stools, excess sweat and urine. Pittas usually have a greater thirst than other doshas.

Spreading – This can be seen in the form of skin rashes, acne, inflammation and heat that moves in the body. Pitta individuals like to be well known and want their name to be spread all over the world.

Oily – They have soft oily skin and hair. They may find it difficult to digest deep-fried foods.

Sour – Pitta can often experience stomach acid, increased reflux and excess salivation.

Pungent – Often Pittas will experience heartburn, or strong burning feelings both physically and mentally. Their bodies may omit a pungent smell either from the mouth, armpits, feet or faeces.

Bitter –They will often be left with a bitter taste in their mouths following heated exchanges. They tend to have an aversion to bitter flavour. They can be bitter and twisted if they don't get their own way.

Red – They can have fiery red hair, flushed red skin, nose and cheeks, red rashes, red skin from sunburn. Red will aggravate Pitta.

Emotions and diet

Pitta females who have not learned to temper their fire can struggle with hot flushes and insomnia during perimenopause and menopause, and this is a time when they need to look closely at the way they are managing their emotions and perhaps question if they are being honest with themselves about how they feel. They may also need to alter their diets and remove heating foods and drinks like red wine, hard cheeses and meats to reduce the fire in the body.

Or they may just stuff any negative emotions down as they present a very competent persona to the outside world.

For Pitta dietary recommendations, see the back of the book, pages 242–3.

Routine and exercise

One of the biggest challenges for Pitta individuals is to slow down and to see life from another person's perspective. Fire governs the eyes in the body so they can often be so focused on what they want and need, forgetting to ask what those around may need and instead assuming they know best.

Because Pitta energy governs the years from 18 to 50–55, it is easy for these types to burn out in their middle years of their life as they tend to push themselves beyond their means both physically and mentally.

Pittas need to avoid overheating so exercising in the middle of the day, especially in summer, is a big no-no. Hot yoga, surfing, sunbaking or any physical work in summer in Pitta hours between 10am and 2pm will not serve them well. Because Pittas like to look good, they can become obsessed with exercise and their body shape, and may become frustrated and moody if their exercise regime is disturbed in any way.

KAPHA

Kapha individuals tend to be heavy set and often experience problems with their weight when they are out of balance. They are calm, caring and compassionate and possess incredible stamina. Kaphas have a strong constitution and tend to live longer than the other doshas.

Elements

- Elements that dominate this dosha – Water and Earth
- Elements that aggravate this dosha – Water and Earth
- Elements that calm this dosha – Fire, Air and Space
- Tastes that aggravate the dosha – sweet, sour, salty
- Tastes that calm the dosha – bitter, pungent, astringent

Time of day

6am–10am and 6pm–10pm. This is the time of day when Kapha will be more obvious in the body and mind.

Time of year

In spring Kapha can be more aggravated in the body. Spring is known as Kapha time (mucus) where we eat light foods, move our body more and shake out any excess weight we have accumulated in winter. This is the season when Kapha types will struggle with respiratory issues, especially a mucus build up; they may struggle losing the extra weight they gained in winter and could even find themselves slipping into depression.

Time of life

0–18 years is the time that Kapha will be more prominent in the body.

Kapha is responsible for compassion, loyalty, patience, forgiveness, body structure (bones, muscles, tendons, ligaments) and stability, lubrication and protection.

KAPHA OUT OF BALANCE

The site of Kapha in the body is the chest, lungs, throat, head, sinuses, nose, mouth and tongue, bones, plasma and mucus, and this is where Kapha will present more strongly when it is out of balance.

Signs that Kapha is out of balance in the body

Lethargy, laziness, difficulty getting out of bed after a good night's sleep, feeling unmotivated, or beginning to isolate yourself and withdraw from friends are signs of imbalance. Kaphas may become greedy and attached or might find themselves overeating or eating for comfort, especially sweet or fatty foods. Weight gain, fluid retention, coughs and colds, slow bowel movements, diabetes, oily skin and hair, congestion in the chest and lungs, excess mucus, asthma, excessive sweet cravings and tender breasts before menstruation are other symptoms Kaphas may experience. Enlarged breasts, emotional eating, watery mucousy blood at period time, long heavy flow, depression and moodiness may also present as symptoms. They might also complain of oily stools that sink and feeling that they have not fully emptied their bowls after going to the toilet.

Kapha types are more likely to go out of balance in spring.

Spring/Kapha health issues: Fluid retention, excess mucus, coughs and colds, slow bowel movements, increased body weight, depression.

Habits and lifestyle factors that imbalance Kapha

Eating too many sweet foods (this includes fruit); eating cold, white, damp foods (especially ice-cream, milk and yoghurt); excess dairy in the diet; too much alcohol or sweet drinks; overeating (especially in the evening before bed); overexposure to cold damp environments, lack of exercise, sleeping during the day and going to bed with wet hair and drinking too much liquid be it water or hot drinks; and sitting around doing nothing for long periods at a time.

Out of balance Kapha individuals can be stubborn, possessive and greedy. Kaphas have a strong attachment to money and will often stay in jobs they are unhappy in if they are making good money.

Environmental effects

The amount of water and earth element in their constitution means they have an aversion to cold damp weather, and if exposed to these conditions for long periods of time, they can develop respiratory issues. Kaphas need to be aware of mould and rising damp in their homes and parents may need to place dehumidifiers in children's rooms during the winter or rainy seasons. Most Kaphas will be much happier and healthier in warmer, drier climates than in cooler, wetter or even humid regions.

KEY Stimulation, variety, good exercise, reduce sweets, stay warm.

AVOID Cold and damp environments, sleeping during the day, sleeping after sunrise, doing nothing, isolation.

BALANCING KAPHA

Activities that will calm Kapha

Vigorous exercise, especially in the morning between 6am–10am, running, cycling, aerobic activity and competitive sports. Learning a new skill, stimulating the mind, changing or varying your daily routine will keep you from feeling stuck and bogged down. Travel, seeking out new friendships and meeting new people – these will get you out of your comfort zone. Have your main meal at lunchtime.

Stimulating remedies – dry brushing or exfoliating self massage with warmed cold pressed sesame oil, energetic exercise that raises a sweat for at least 30 minutes per day (think running, cycling, yoga or hiking) drinking hot water and lemon with a small pinch of cayenne on waking to stimulate digestion, keeping warm, and standing at one's desk instead of sitting.

Stimulating lifestyle choices – listening to music or audio that stimulates the mind, walking rather than driving, socialising instead of choosing to be alone.

So-called healthy foods that may increase the mucus and dampness in the body – yoghurt, cheese, bananas, smoothies, acai bowls, chilled drinks, fruit juices, green smoothies.

HOW KAPHA MANIFESTS IN THE BODY

Heavy – Kaphas have heavy bones with solid frames, bulky muscles and can be overweight, they have calm deep voices and are usually quite grounded in mind and body.

Slow/Dull – They can tend to be slow to react, they walk and speak slowly, and only speak after allowing time to think about what they are going to say. Kaphas have a sluggish metabolism.

Cool – They have cold clammy skin, they often get a cold, cough or congestion, and they are drawn to cooling sweet foods.

Oily – They have soft oily skin, hair and faeces and well-lubricated joints.

Liquid – Kaphas tend to have a problem with fluid retention, congestion in their chest, nose and throat, and excess mucus; this can be very obvious in young children with runny noses.

Smooth – Blessed with soft smooth alabaster like skin and a smooth calm nature.

Dense – This quality ensures Kaphas have thick hair, nails, skin and muscles.

Soft – They have soft doe-like eyes and a very soft caring nature, which makes them extremely forgiving.

Static – This unfortunately can make them very happy sitting around, sleeping for long periods of time.

Sticky – They can have a tendency to become quite attached to things they care about.

Cloudy – Kaphas can have a foggy mind in the morning, they can also take a while to understand things at the best of times.

Hard – This quality gives the firm muscles and strength in both mind and body.

Gross – Kaphas can suffer from fatty tissue, blockages and obesity.

Sweet – These people have a sweet nature, and are also drawn to sweet foods that can cause them to become unbalanced.

Salty – Salty taste will assist in digestion, however, too much salt can lead to fluid retention and this can often be a problem for Kaphas.

White – Kaphas have a pale complexion, they love white food especially dairy.

Lifestyle factors to limit – Too much sitting, excess exposure to damp and cold, lying around watching movies for extended periods and spending too much time alone.

Emotions and diet

Kaphas move slowly, speak slowly and don't like being forced into making quick decisions. They have stable minds and a solid sense of self, but out of balance they can struggle with long episodes of depression and melancholy. These are very private individuals and often suffer alone, making everyone's problems more important than their own. Kaphas' first step in addressing their emotions is admitting to what they are feeling, as they often minimise their emotions or laugh them off. Giving themselves permission to cry or show their vulnerability to those they trust is a big thing for Kaphas, who tend to soldier on regardless.

Kapha types love sweet foods and will be the people who crave ice-cream or a sweet treat after dinner. Indulging in habits like this will only lead to weight gain, excess mucus and negative feelings about themselves.

For food that suits Kaphas, see the charts at the back of the book, pages 244–5.

Routine and exercise

For Kapha types to lead balanced lives, they need to challenge themselves and get out of their comfort zones. Often found talking about wanting to begin an exercise or weight-loss program, they need to just start. Once they start something they are the most dedicated and consistent of all the doshas and blessed with strong bodies that have great endurance.

They are natural earth mothers and some may find it difficult to let their children grow up and lead independent lives. Kaphas need to spend more time focusing on themselves and less on others.

Ayurveda is the science that indicates the appropriate and inappropriate, happy or sorrowful conditions of living, what is auspicious or inauspicious for longevity, as well as the measure of life itself.

– Charaka Samhita 1.41

STAGES OF LIFE AND AYURVEDIC SEASONS

It is not only food that affects our constitutions; the environment, time of day, time of year and the weather also have an effect. Certain elements are more dominant in our body at certain times of our lives, to the point where they can dominate or strongly affect our health. These phases (also known as stages) are also named, a little confusingly, as doshas. So you could be a Vata dosha going through a Kapha phase of life in Pitta weather (summer). See more about seasonal eating in The Ayurvedic approach to health chapter (pages 42–6). If you are a blend of doshas or tridoshic (a balance of all three) this could become even more complicated, especially if you are cooking for a family with mixed doshas.

These stages of life are described beautifully in ancient Ayurvedic texts.

Kapha stage: 0 to 18 years – Student

Pitta stage: 18 to 50–55 years – Householder

Pitta Vata stage: 50–55 to 75 years – Hermitage

Vata stage: 75 years to death – Renunciation

The years in each stage are not fixed and will vary with each individual.

The Kapha stage is known as the 'student' phase of life as this is a time of learning and discovering boundaries and discipline. It is a time for building knowledge and intellect along with new tissues in the body. Mucus is the by-product of the manufacture of tissue and this is why young children, no matter what dosha they are, always seem to have an issue with mucus.

The Pitta phase can actually be divided into two phases. The first part of the Pitta phase is referred to as the 'householder' years where the focus of one's life is on making your mark in the world, meeting a partner, creating a home and raising a family. This fire stage is mainly about working hard and building wealth, and we use the momentum and heat created in the body in these years to help us stay focused on the job at hand, and during this period we may feel more confident, sociable and ambitious. Because there is more heat in the body during these years we may also suffer with insomnia, skin issues, heartburn, stomach ulcers and hypertension.

The second half of the Pitta phase, also known as the Pitta Vata phase, is often referred to as the 'hermitage' stage and happens after 50 or 55 years where people start to let go of the attachments to money and fame and become more involved in helping others or focusing on their retirement. People may move to a quieter area and choose to live a simpler life but they are still available to family and their community for help and advice. During this phase people may show signs of both Pitta and Vata imbalance.

The Vata stage is known as the 'renunciation' stage where we are preparing for death. I know that sounds a little morbid but it can be an incredibly special time in one's life. People in this phase, even if very mentally and physically active, start to become progressively more inward looking and less concerned with what is happening in the world around them; their body is now dominated by Vata so it becomes drier and colder and their digestion slows down. Joints may ache and they may become more forgetful, anxious and fearful.

The transition is slow and happens over several years, and people develop at different ages and stages. If we try to fight against these stages, it will quickly create imbalances in our bodies. In some ways the refusal of people in the west to gracefully accept and honour ageing and its natural phases could be seen as the cause of many of the health issues we are seeing today.

Issues that may arise during the Kapha years: stomach problems, congested lungs, blocked sinuses, runny noses.

Issues that may arise during the Pitta years: skin problems, acne, infection, inflammation, blood issues, headaches, migraines, liver problems, bile.

Issues that may arise during the Vata years: negativity around ageing, loss of flexibility and strength in the body, memory loss, dryness, loss of direction, osteoporosis, frailty, weakness of the immune system, joint pain.

Now that you know your dosha, or doshas, you can begin to work to nourish and look after yourself according to it and the stage of life you are in as well as being more aware of why you might be more susceptible to certain environments, seasons, changes to the weather and foods than others.

Added to that, I always recommend that people are mindful of the signs of Vata imbalance. We all have some level of Vata imbalance these days, which is the direct result of living busy lives in which we are exposed to way too much Vata unbalancing technology – phones, computers, ipads etc.

The main thing about this book is that you learn how to familiarise yourself with what isn't working for you. If your doshas are strongly out of balance, then you may need to follow the chapter set aside for the dosha that is out of balance until you come back into balance and then you can return to following an eating and lifestyle regime that is more in line with your own constitution. (See page 22 for Vata, page 27 for Pitta and page 31 for Kapha.)

The Ayurvedic approach to health

It's not about the food we eat, it's about the food we digest.

Ayurvedic practitioner Dr Robert Svoboda

One of the main aims of Ayurveda is to help us achieve a balanced relationship with the environment that we live in. Eating seasonal, local produce is one of the easiest ways to manage your health. Developing an awareness of how your digestive system is functioning is one of the best ways to monitor your own health. How we metabolise, digest and eliminate our food is a great diagnostic tool for how our body is functioning. To help keep the body in an optimal state of health, Ayurveda has developed daily routines that are recommended for each dosha. It also recommends periods of cleansing and fasting for certain doshas in specific seasons.

SEASONAL EATING

I find that because we are usually a combination of two doshas the best way to cover the food part is to be very mindful of the seasons. The doshas are dominated by the yearly seasons. In summer follow a Pitta style eating plan (designed to cool fiery Pittas in the hottest season), in autumn and early winter a Vata style eating plan (designed to settle and ground skittish Vatas in the most changeable seasons) and in late winter and spring a Kapha-style eating plan (designed to warm and dry out watery, slow moving Kaphas and put some bounce in their step). This way you will find that you can still have a variety of foods in your diet and you can enjoy all of the recipes in this book.

Remember that each dosha is a little more fragile in the season that they are dominated by, so a Pitta will be more likely to get overheated in summer, a Kapha more mucousy and chesty in spring and a Vata more anxious and likely to experience tummy issues in autumn and early winter. This will work really well for you if you are in a good state of health and is a lovely way of experiencing the different feelings within a season.

DIGESTION AND ELIMINATION

Digestion and elimination are used as a diagnostic tool in Ayurveda and pretty much everything in Ayurveda stems from how we digest the food we eat. If you have ever been to see an Ayurvedic practitioner you will remember being asked lots of private questions about your poo, wee, gas, sweating and, if you are a woman, your menstrual cycle. Then you will have been asked to poke out your tongue, which is another method of determining your state of health.

I realise talking about these things may make you feel uncomfortable. That's OK. I just want you to understand that the more familiar you are with how your body processes the food you eat, the more in touch with your digestive system you will become. Ayurveda states that the health of the digestive system determines the state of wellness of the whole body. Modern science is now also starting to recognise how significant gut health is.

To understand how we evaluate digestive health in Ayurveda you need to learn about a few key concepts.

AGNI AND AMA – THE KEY TO DIGESTIVE HEALTH

Agni is the word used to describe digestive fire in Ayurveda. The strength of one's agni is one of the biggest factors in determining someone's overall health.

Ama is a build up of toxins we get in our body if we have low digestive fire or poor agni. This then creates a vicious cycle where ama reduces agni and low agni produces more ama. The main cause of ama is improper eating habits. Signs of ama build-up are very similar to those of low agni.

Ama is a Sanskrit word meaning uncooked or unripe. As ama is usually a result of low digestive fire caused from eating too much raw or uncooked food, Ayurveda recommends that people favour cooked food over raw food, especially in the cooler months and especially if they have more fragile digestive systems. Both Vata and Kapha doshas often suffer with digestive issues as they don't have as much digestive fire as Pitta types.

Eating cooling or raw foods in the hours between 6am–10am and 6pm–10pm when the Kapha phase is dominant will further compromise anyone's digestive system. This is why Ayurveda recommends eating our biggest meals in the middle of the day between 10am and 2pm, which is the Pitta phase of the day when our digestive fire is at its peak. Developing healthy habits such as these will help rekindle the digestive fire and reduce the amount of ama in the system. Ama can be removed from the digestive system quickly and efficiently through diet, but once it moves deeper into the other tissues of the body it becomes more problematic, as it weakens our ability to respond to disease and infections. That is why in Ayurveda we are always checking in on the digestive system and evaluating how we are processing the food we eat.

Signs of ama build-up

- White coating on the back of the tongue
- Inability to focus
- Constipation, lymph congestion
- Fatigue, sluggishness, lethargy
- Loss of sexual desire

- Poor appetite, loss of taste
- Indigestion, heartburn, diarrhoea
- Stagnation
- Gas, bloating

Causes of ama build-up

- Overeating
- Snacking between meals
- Incompatible food combinations (see page 63)
- Too much raw or uncooked foods
- Too much sugar in the diet
- Excess heavy, fatty or fried foods
- Excess processed foods
- Too many sweet, sour or salty foods
- Eating late and going to bed with undigested food in the stomach
- Eating when stressed or emotional
- Not sleeping properly
- Lack of exercise
- Drinking while eating
- Continued stress over long periods of time
- Not dealing with emotional issues
- Eating irregular meals, skipping meals
- Eating when not hungry
- Drinking fruit juice with a meal
- Eating at the wrong time of day, either too early or too late
- Eating when constipated

ELIMINATION

When we sleep, our body is digesting the food we have eaten, so when we wake our bodies should be ready to eliminate the waste from the night before. Our body has several areas through which it can eliminate – through the bowel, the urine, the skin, the blood and the mouth.

The Ayurvedic daily routine recommends scraping your tongue to remove any ama that has built up on the tongue overnight. Next we go to the toilet, emptying the bowel and bladder; if we are not pooing and peeing on waking it indicates that there is some sluggishness in the digestive system and it would be wise to address this sooner rather than later. Healthy elimination is vitally important.

What healthy elimination looks like

Go to the toilet 1–2 times per day to poo, ideally once as soon as you wake up. You should have no pain or discomfort and your poo should be the consistency of a ripe banana and similar shape (not necessarily the length). It should float, not smell unpleasant and be light brown in colour.

Each dosha has a distinct way of showing us it is out of balance. See Balancing the doshas, page 22.

Circadian rhythms and daily routine

Our bodies are programmed to live in accordance with the natural rhythms of nature but somehow we seem to have become disconnected from these. More and more people are finding they are no longer rising with the sun and resting as the sun goes down. Increased exposure to technology at home has seen people now working into the early hours of the morning on their computers and children spending hours on their phones at night, and as a direct result of this there has been a rise in folks struggling to get a restful night's sleep. In Ayurveda, we prescribe a daily routine to help maintain our relationship with nature's circadian rhythms. The routine below can be followed by all doshas.

DAILY ROUTINE FOR ALL DOSHAS

Morning
Wake before sunrise. Spit and scrape your tongue using a copper or stainless steel tongue scraper, then drink a cup of hot water (with 1 tablespoon lemon juice if lemons are in season). Brush your teeth with a good quality, natural sugar-free toothpaste or powder. Go to the toilet – poo and pee within the first hour of waking. Before your shower, practise yoga or gentle stretches for 15–30 minutes or go for a brisk 30-minute walk, followed by 15 minutes of meditation or mindful breathing. After this, swish some coconut or sesame oil around your mouth for about 5–10 minutes to remove any toxins from the mouth. This is called 'oil pulling' and helps maintain a healthy balance of microbes in the mouth and gums. End the pre-breakfast morning routine with some self massage (abyhanga), see page 50.

Breakfast
Eat a small amount of breakfast: enough to get you to lunch without a snack. Pittas tend to have a larger appetite and faster metabolism than Vata and Kapha types. Kapha types have the slowest metabolism so they can even benefit from having a light breakfast or a simple drink. Ayurveda does not recommend snacking; it likes to give your body time to digest the food you have eaten before your next meal. Pittas and Vatas will tolerate snacking more than Kaphas.

Lunch
Make this your biggest meal of the day – this can be eaten between 10am and 2pm. Take a gentle walk to stimulate digestion. Depending on your dosha you may want to take a short rest after lunch. Sleeping in the middle of the day is not recommended for Kapha types.

Evening
Have an early light dinner around 6.30pm–7pm followed by gentle evening exercise, breathing exercises or meditation. Aim to be in bed by 9.30pm with lights out by 10pm. Avoid having devices in your bedroom.

WHY FOLLOW THIS ROUTINE?

I recognise that this routine may not be possible for everyone every day. Try to do what you can when you can and you will feel the benefits.

Ayurveda has developed this routine to align with the doshas and nature. Exercise is recommended between 6am and 10am as this is when the Kapha dosha is at its strongest and the body may feel a little sluggish. Eating the biggest meal of the day is favoured between 10am and 2pm as this is when the Pitta digestive properties are optimal. Resting or doing focussed mental work between 2pm and 6pm is ideal as this is when Vata's nervous system is heightened. The nervous system requires calming before the simple evening meal and slow-down period before bed.

The main part of the routine is the morning tongue scrape, lemon water and mindfulness. The resting in the middle of the day is more of a weekend thing but it is important to remember to take time out for lunch and a break in the middle of the day. An early dinner and lights out before 10pm is ideal.

Why have hot water or hot lemon and water in the morning?

Lemons are a seasonal fruit so when they are not in season just enjoy a cup of hot water on waking; it will still stimulate and warm the digestive system and relieve thirst. A hot lemon drink is considered easy to digest and to stimulate agni (digestive fire). It can also relieve a cough and can relieve colic and abdominal pain.

Be aware that unripe lemon is sour and decreases Vata and Kapha but increases Pitta if consumed in excess and ripe lemon decreases Pitta and Kapha but can increase Vata in excess.

A glass of hot lemon water in the morning is recommended for all body types but is especially beneficial for Kaphas who are looking to shed excess weight as it is said to decrease fat deposition. I also recommend adding a pinch of cayenne to this as it will further assist in increasing digestive fire.

Why do we tongue scrape?

While we are sleeping our body is digesting and using all its methods of elimination to remove anything it no longer needs from the body. Built-up toxins (ama) accumulate on the surface of the tongue overnight and when we wake we need to remove them from the tongue before we start the day.

I use a copper tongue scraper because copper is an antiseptic, antibacterial metal and helps increase the enzymes in your mouth that encourage the growth of good bacteria. You can purchase copper tongue scrapers from health food stores or online. If you cannot find a copper tongue scraper, a stainless steel one is absolutely fine too but it won't have the same properties as a copper one. I scrape my tongue 7–10 times gently. I am not trying to scrape my taste buds off!

Before scraping your tongue, look at your tongue carefully to see how your body is working. As soon as you wake up, spit and then poke your tongue out and see what is on the surface and what colour it is, and then scrape your tongue before brushing your teeth.

To scrape your tongue, hold the tongue scraper in two hands and scrape down the centre from the back of your tongue to the front, then the two sides back to the front and then the centre again. Rinse in between, then repeat. Start as far back on your tongue as you can; you are trying to remove as much of the thick furry coating as possible. If this bacteria is left in the mouth on the tongue, it can cause bad breath, gum disease and tooth decay; removing it will improve your sense of taste.

INDICATIONS OF TONGUE HEALTH

COLOUR		OTHER FEATURES ON THE TONGUE	
RED	Excess Pitta	TREMORS	Disturbance in the nervous system, anxiety, fear
BROWN AND DRY	Excess Vata	CRACK AT THE TIP	Problems in the cervical spine
WHITE WITH SOME MUCUS	Excess Kapha	CRACK DOWN THE CENTRE	Problem with the spine or deep emotional disturbance
WHITE OR YELLOWISH COATING	Undigested food or ama	BITE MARKS ON THE TONGUE	Malabsorption of nutrients

If you are depressed you are living in the past

If you are anxious you are living in the future

If you are at peace you are living in the present

–Lao Tzu

SELF MASSAGE

Self massage, or abhyanga as we call it in Ayurveda, is one of the most beautiful rituals in the daily routine. We massage the body daily to help remove toxins from the body, move energy and help the body heal. It is said to benefit the endocrine, lymphatic and nervous systems. The quality of the oil you use is really important so please don't be stingy with this. Warming the oil is recommended if you live in a colder climate; in summer I don't bother, but in winter coconut oil will be solid at room temperature so you will need to, and it also feels wonderful when it is applied to the skin warm. Make sure the room is warm and there is no draught.

What oil?

Each dosha has an oil that is recommended for them.

Vata – organic cold pressed sesame or almond oil or a medicated Ayurvedic oil

Pitta – organic cold pressed coconut oil or Brahmi oil

Kapha – organic cold pressed sesame oil and use less than other doshas

A note about sesame oil. First, it is not toasted sesame oil. Secondly, it stains so you need to apply it before a shower and then use an old towel to rub off any excess.

The method

It is best done in the morning or before bed if mornings won't work for you. Allow 5–10 minutes and allow yourself to be present, as this is a really nurturing thing you can do for yourself. You can sit or stand to apply the oil. I always sit on the edge of my bath but I make sure I am standing on a bath mat so any oil can drip onto that. I use a squeeze bottle and use about ¼ cup per massage.

Start at the head. Massage the hair with oil once a week only. Using circular motions, massage the face, then in and around the ears. Use long strokes on the neck and shoulders and continue down the arms from the outside of the body in. Use circular strokes around the joints. Massage the torso and chest in a circular motion. On the belly, massage up the right side and over to the left and down in a clockwise direction (following the path of the large intestine to support healthy bowel function). Massage your sides with long strokes and the hips with circular strokes. Use long strokes on the legs, outside first and then inside. Finish with the feet, using long strokes and circular motions on the sole of the foot, toes and heels. Be careful now as your feet will be slippery. Shower, then rub off any excess oil using an old towel or pop on a pair of socks.

Why do we do self massage?

It softens, moisturises and warms or cools the skin depending on the oil you use. Coconut oil cools the skin for Pitta types, and sesame oil warms the skin for the cooler Vata and Kapha types. Self massage limits or helps reduce the effects of ageing, stimulates circulation and tones internal organs, and improves sleep. It also helps restore cracked dry feet and stimulate blood flow to the lower limbs, tones muscles, and removes toxins and build up in the lymph nodes.

When to avoid self massage

- During the menstrual cycle
- If the skin is broken, burnt or damaged
- If there is any type of clot or swelling that cannot be explained
- If you have any type of serious medical condition including fevers, chills, flu or allergic reactions
- If you are pregnant, consult your doctor; no detoxing therapies while carrying a baby.

Hygiene and safety

Cleaning off the oil is important, especially if you're using sesame: use an old towel to do this. Add shampoo to hair before rinsing oil out of your hair with water. Wash the bathtub or shower out afterwards as this will help stop the oil building up in your pipes. Wash towels with a bit of bicarbonate soda and vinegar.

MEDITATION

I'm not going to write a whole lot here about meditation, but I will say that if you have a busy mind, sitting still and trying to quieten your mind is a good way to drive yourself nuts or get to see just how busy your mind can be. It's like going on a diet and then feeling hungrier than ever before.

I meditate for about 10–20 minutes morning and night but I use an app on my phone and listen to guided meditations. These give me clear concise instructions about aligning my breath and I find my mind naturally lets go and softens once I place my focus on the breath.

You may choose to just sit quietly and focus on your breath. There are many methods of meditation, so find one that works for you. Start with 5 minutes and then build up over time. Try not to get too attached to doing 20 minutes every day, as life is always changing and you need to be able to change with it.

Four things necessary to practise meditation:

1. A quiet space

2. Enough room to sit or lie comfortably

3. Something to focus on – mantra, breath or a guided meditation

4. A lack of self-judgement

Meditation is something that will change your life in subtle ways, so don't expect too much from it in the early stages. Simply setting aside time for yourself to be still and breathe at the beginning and end of your day will make a big difference to your state of health.

CLEANSING AND FASTING

Ayurveda has recommended periods of cleansing and fasting for many moons now. These practices need to be approached with caution, however, as they are not suited to all doshas. It is wise to consult your GP or health practitioner before embarking on any of the regimes discussed here.

Cleansing, fasting, juicing and detoxing have been buzzwords for a few years now and there seems to be a little confusion about what is what.

Fasting involves not eating for 12 hours or more; water or herbal tea is taken but nothing more. If I have a particularly big month of recipe testing and tasting, I may choose to fast one day a week to give my system a break. I am a Pitta and if I choose this when I am stressed, things can get ugly as Pittas usually have a pretty big appetite, so sipping on water or herbal tea in summer when my digestive fire is on overdrive is a pretty stupid thing for me to do. However, if I choose to fast for one day a week in winter when the food I have been eating is heavier, and my entire system is a little less fiery, I feel fantastic.

People fast for spiritual and religious reasons or these days people are intermittently fasting, which means not eating for several hours between meals, as it is believed to be an effective weight loss tool. Ayurveda has always recommended eating an early light supper and then eating nothing until the morning, which is basically the same thing.

Fasting is not recommended for Vata types. Their digestive systems are fragile and because of this they need to eat regular meals. Vatas are aggravated by too much air and space in the body, so too much time between meals can be very unbalancing for them. I hope you are starting to get the picture. This is all about making choices that suit your body type and reflect how you are feeling from day to day. Kaphas can benefit from fasting as they have the slowest metabolism of all the doshas.

Juice fasting involves drinking only juices – usually a combination of fruit and vegetable juices. Be careful with the ratio of fruit to vegetables in your juices as too much fruit can lead to spikes and falls in your blood sugar levels, leaving you feeling light-headed and nauseous. A ratio of 7:3 vegetables to fruit is ideal.

Juice fasts are suitable for Kaphas with very sluggish digestive systems or Pittas with strong digestive fires and then only in the warmer months. Winter is not a time for juice fasting. Vata types need to be very careful when it comes to juice fasts and I would not recommend that they embark on one without consulting an Ayurvedic practitioner or naturopath first.

CLEANSING OR DETOXING

Cleansing or detoxing involves eating foods that are easy on your digestive system. It is done to cleanse the digestive system of toxins (ama) that may have built up as a result of unhealthy eating habits or poor food combinations. A cleanse can last from one day up to 28 days and should be approached with caution.

I like to cleanse in spring after eating heavier foods in winter. I usually do a 1–2 week cleanse with my yoga students. I have been doing this for about 15 years now and I find it is a perfect reset for me. I will also put myself on a cleanse if I've overindulged in the festive season. I'm in no way fanatical about cleansing and I do it as a way of being kind to myself, not as a punishment. I will also choose to do a cleanse as a reset if I am eating too much sugar or just not making the right food choices I know I need to. I really enjoy taking all of the naughty stuff away for a bit and getting back to lovely simple flavours. Kitchari (see page 56 for the recipe) is one of my favourite things in the whole world, so too are steamed vegetables and broth-style soups so I don't find cleansing a chore.

Once you have done a few cleanses I'm pretty certain you will start to feel the same way. One thing I learnt early on in my cleansing years was to be mindful about how I break my cleanse. It is important to ease back into foods you have moved away from; you may feel tempted to celebrate your end of cleanse with something naughty, but it is not recommended. That's not to say I haven't done so in the past and won't do so in the future. Remember we are aiming for progress, not perfection!

The right fast or cleanse for you

Often people think they are doing something great for themselves spending 1 week on a juice fast in winter, but if you are a Vata body type, then this is possibly the worst thing you could do for yourself. The main thing we are looking to do in Ayurveda through a fast is to rekindle our digestive fire – agni.

Signs you might need to cleanse or fast

- Digestive issues of any kind
- Constipation, loose stools, gas, bloating, irregular bowel movements
- Cravings for sweet, sour or salty flavours that are intense and hard to ignore
- You are unaware of what your body wants or needs when it comes to sleep, rest, exercise
- You feel cloudy or find it difficult to listen and focus
- You find yourself feeling heavy and retaining fluid

- Anxiety and stress are running you
- Sleep is a major issue for you, either you have trouble getting to sleep or you wake up and can't get back to sleep
- You feel emotional, distracted and annoyed by the smallest things
- You can't put your finger on it but you just don't feel right
- You find it hard to get out of bed in the morning, feeling unmotivated and depressed

Why cleanse?

Cleansing gives the digestive system a break and draws the ama (toxins) and excess Vata, Pitta and Kapha out of the tissues and into the digestive tract, where they can be eliminated.

Which cleanse?

The main principle of cleansing is to give your digestive system a break and the easiest way to do this is to eat less and make what you are eating very easy to digest.

You are looking to balance the Vata, Pitta and Kapha energies in the body, eliminate toxins and most importantly strengthen your digestive agni.

In Ayurveda we usually start with a one-day kitchari fast, or if you are a Kapha type who feels very heavy and sluggish you might want to do a one-day green juice cleanse (see page 60).

ONE DAY KITCHARI CLEANSE

Please do not embark on the cleanse if you are pregnant, breastfeeding, are very weak or are recovering from any recent illness.

This is a gentle cleanse that is suitable for all body types.

- You eat three small meals (about 1 cup) of tridoshic kitchari for one day, making the last meal of your day before 7pm.

- Sip on hot water or the coriander, cumin and fennel tea to help support the digestive system. These spices are known in Ayurveda to be specific digestive spices.

- You want to consume about 2 litres of liquid during the day. You can have a combination of water or digestive tea in the day; this will help flush the toxins out of your system. It is important that you avoid drinking with meals.

- You can do gentle exercise on a cleanse day but it is not advised that you do strenuous exercise.

Routine for kitchari cleanse day

- ☐ Wake and scrape tongue, brush teeth
- ☐ Drink 1 cup of warm water or digestive tea
- ☐ Meditation and gentle exercise
- ☐ Body massage or dry brush
- ☐ Shower
- ☐ **Breakfast:** 1 cup tridoshic kitchari
- ☐ 30 minutes after breakfast: 1–2 cups digestive tea or water
- ☐ No food until lunch
- ☐ **Lunch:** 1 cup tridoshic kitchari
- ☐ 30 minutes after lunch: 1–2 cups digestive tea or water
- ☐ No food until dinner
- ☐ **Dinner:** 1 cup tridoshic kitchari
- ☐ 30 minutes after dinner: 1 cup digestive tea
- ☐ Gentle walk or yoga
- ☐ Warm water or digestive tea before bed
- ☐ Scrape tongue, brush teeth
- ☐ In bed by 9.30pm and lights out before 10pm

Tridoshic kitchari

In this recipe it is important to use easy-to-digest in-season vegetables that are tridoshic, which means they can be tolerated by all the doshas. Ensure you use a good quality salt. Salt is an important ingredient when cleansing as it helps balance the electrolytes in the body and provides us with energy.

Soak the rice and dhal in cold water overnight. Rinse and drain well.

Heat the ghee in a large non-stick frying pan, add the ghee and spices and cook over medium heat for 2 minutes, or until the spices are fragrant and golden.

Add the rice and dhal and cook for 3 minutes or until coated with the ghee. Add the vegetables and water and bring to boil. Boil uncovered for 5 minutes or until obvious tunnels appear in the rice, reduce heat to a simmer, cover and cook for 10 minutes, or until the rice is soft and most of the liquid has been absorbed. Remove from the heat, add a squeeze of lemon, garnish with coriander and season with salt.

I make this recipe in the morning and eat it for the rest of the day. Ayurveda is not a fan of leftovers so this is why I choose to cleanse with my yoga students or buddy up with a friend. It's great to have someone to share what comes up for you when you take away those food crutches that can often be covering up some tricky emotions.

1 cup (200 g) organic basmati rice
½ cup (110 g) organic split mung beans (moong dhal)
2 tablespoons organic ghee
1 teaspoon cumin seeds
1 teaspoon fennel seeds
1 teaspoon organic ground turmeric
1 teaspoon ground coriander
2 zucchinis, grated
2 carrots, grated
200 g green beans
3–4 cups water
juice of 1 lemon
handful of chopped fresh coriander
pinch of salt

Digestive tea

Place the seeds into a pan, add the water and bring to boil.

Reduce heat and simmer for 10 minutes, strain and serve warm or at room temperature.

1 teaspoon coriander seeds
1 teaspoon cumin seeds
1 teaspoon fennel seeds
3 cups water

ONE DAY GREEN JUICE CLEANSE

Follow the routine on pg 56 but replace the kitchari with the green juice.

As a Pitta, juice fasting is not something I am a fan of but it is good for Kapha types, especially in spring. As their metabolism is naturally slower than the other two doshas, they may feel the desire to eat less and give their digestive system a rest after they have eaten a lot. There are broth and green juice recipes in Food Medicine (pages 213–27). Remember, warming foods are best to cleanse with in cooler months and juices are more suited to warmer days or when your body is feeling as though it has had too much of a good thing and it needs a break.

Kapha green juice

Make sure all ingredients are at room temperature. This juice is best consumed in spring and summer.

Push the fruit through a juicer and drink.

1 apple
juice of 1 lime
2 stalks celery
½ cup (100 g) berries, not frozen
3cm piece fresh ginger, roughly chopped
2cm piece fresh turmeric, roughly chopped
a handful of organic spinach or kale

Simple green juice

Put ingredients into a blender and blend until smooth and creamy.

2 handfuls green grapes
2 handfuls green spinach
½ teaspoon ground ginger
½ cup (125 ml) water

Possession of material riches, without inner peace,
is like dying of thirst while bathing in a lake.

–Paramahansa Yogananda

Food combining

Ayurveda considers the way food is combined as important as the food you choose.

I want you to take these recommendations lightly. Sometimes we are unable to control the food we eat and in these cases I encourage you to let it go and make the healthiest choice you can. These are only suggestions. For example, you may find you can eat fruit and yoghurt for the rest of your life without ever experiencing any issues at all.

INCOMPATIBLE AND SUPPORTIVE FOOD COMBINATIONS

FOOD	INCOMPATIBLE WITH	SUPPORTIVE COMBINATION
BEANS	Fruit, cheese, eggs, fish, milk, yoghurt	Grains, vegetables, nuts and seeds
EGGS	Fruit, especially melons, beans, cheese, fish, kitchari, milk, yoghurt	
FRUIT	Avoid combining with other foods; exceptions are dates and milk and some cooked fruits	
GRAINS	Fruit	Beans, vegetables, eggs, meat, fish, nuts, seeds, cheese, yoghurt
HONEY	Honey should never be boiled or cooked, nor be mixed in equal quantities with ghee	
LEMON	Cucumber, milk, tomatoes, yoghurt; lime can be used with tomatoes and yoghurt	Suitable in moderation with other foods
MELONS	Avoid combining with other foods, especially dairy, eggs, fried foods, grains Melons are hard to digest and really should be eaten alone	
MILK	Bananas (milk and banana is a difficult combination for the body to digest – yet it is the base of a smoothie!); cherries, melons, sour fruits, bread containing yeast, fish, kitchari, meat, yoghurt	Milk is best eaten alone and heated with warming spices; it can be eaten with rice, dates, almonds and warm with porridge (oats)
VEGETABLES	Fruit and milk	Grains, nuts, seeds, fish, meat, yoghurt, cheese, eggs
NIGHTSHADES – CAPSICUM, EGGPLANT, POTATO AND TOMATO	Melon, cucumber, milk, cheese, yoghurt	Vegetables, beans, grains, meat, fish, nuts, seeds
YOGHURT	Fruit, cheese, eggs, fish, hot drinks, meat, beans, nightshades and especially not milk and hot drinks	Vegetables and grains
CHEESE	Fruit, beans, eggs, milk, yoghurt, hot drinks	Grains, vegetables
BUTTER AND GHEE	Butter may not be combined with many foods because of its milk solids; ghee is a much healthier choice when it comes to food combining	Ghee with grains, milk, vegetables, nuts, seeds, fish, meat, egg, cooked fruit

Vata Recipes

AUTUMN, EARLY WINTER VATA SEASON

At this time of year all doshas will do well to favour warm grounding foods. Vata types, in particular, will need to reduce those cooling foods you may have been able to enjoy in summer. Let go of your morning smoothies and replace them with warming cooked breakfasts. You will want to start adding ghee to everything to calm and ground your Vata as the winds that whip up in autumn and early winter can start to unnerve you. Adding warm spices to all your meals is recommended. Vatas may feel more anxious, fearful and vulnerable in these seasons and this is normal. Now is the time you need to pay particular attention to your mind and your digestion.

The recipes in this chapter are suitable for Vata types or those who feel they have a Vata imbalance.

Symptoms of a Vata imbalance include anxiety, tremors, constipation, inability to focus, gas and bloating.

All doshas are easily affected by Vata, so if you are feeling a little unsettled and off colour, make friends with the following recipes as they will be of benefit.

Breakfast

It is important for Vata types to take time to sit down and eat breakfast. Starting the day in a calm, relaxed way will set the tone for their day. Skipping meals is not recommended for Vatas as it just aggravates their sensitive constitutions. Warm cooked breakfasts are a great choice for Vata types. The sweet flavour helps balance this dosha so eating fruit and warming sweet spices is recommended.

Papaya frushie

This is one of my favourite brekkie recipes I tested for this book. Think of it as fruit sushi.

Make sure your fruit is sweet and ripe and try to have it at room temperature – eating chilled, sour, unripe fruit aggravates Vata.

Place the sushi rice and 2 cups of water in a saucepan, bring to the boil and cook over high heat for 5 minutes, until tunnels start to appear in the rice. Reduce the heat to low, cover, and cook for 10 minutes, until the rice is soft.

Add the coconut cream, maple syrup and vanilla to the rice and gently mix to combine.

Spoon the coconut rice into the papaya boats, then top with the fruit.

Serves 4

½ cup (105 g) sushi rice

1 cup (250 ml) coconut cream

1 teaspoon pure maple syrup

1 teaspoon vanilla powder or natural vanilla extract

2 small red papayas, peeled, halved and seeds removed

1 mango, thinly sliced

1 star fruit, thinly sliced

3 passionfruit

Banana blueberry pancakes

The batter for these simple gluten-free pancakes can be made the night before and left in the fridge, ready to be cooked the next morning.

Place the mashed banana in a food processor or blender with the tahini, beaten egg, almond meal and cinnamon. Process or blend until smooth. Transfer the mixture to a jug. Cover and leave the batter to rest for 30 minutes, or overnight. The batter will thicken on standing.

Stir the blueberries into the batter.

Heat 1 tablespoon of coconut oil in a large non-stick frying pan over medium heat, then add 3 tablespoons of batter per pancake and cook in batches of four for 2 minutes, until the underside is golden and bubbles appear on the surface. Turn and cook the other side for 2 minutes, until golden. Remove the pancakes from the pan, place on a plate and keep warm. Add a little more coconut oil to the pan and repeat with the remaining batter until you have 12 pancakes in total.

Stack the pancakes on serving plates and finish with a drizzle of honey.

Serves 4

3 very ripe bananas (490 g), mashed

¼ cup (65 g) hulled tahini

6 eggs, lightly beaten

1 cup (120 g) almond meal

½ teaspoon ground cinnamon

1 cup (200 g) fresh blueberries

3 tablespoons extra-virgin coconut oil

2 tablespoons raw honey

Coconut chia porridge

A simple warming porridge that is perfect for winter. In the warmer months you could serve this chilled.

Place the chia seeds in a frying pan, add the coconut cream, coconut, cinnamon, cardamom and ginger and cook, stirring, over medium heat for 5 minutes, until the mixture thickens slightly.

Remove the pan from the heat, stir in the ghee and maple syrup.

Divide the mixture between four serving bowls, top with Ghee-baked fruit (page 72) and a little of the cooking juices.

Serves 4

½ cup (80 g) chia seeds

1 x 400 ml can coconut cream

½ cup (45 g) desiccated coconut

1 teaspoon ground cinnamon

1 teaspoon ground cardamom

½ teaspoon ground ginger

2 tablespoons ghee

1 tablespoon pure maple syrup

Vegan pumpkin bread with spiced walnuts

Be warned: this is one of those loaves that is nearly impossible to stop at just one slice. Make sure you roast your pumpkin; if you boil it, the bread will be too moist.

Preheat the oven to 180°C. Grease and line the base and sides of a 20 cm x 10 cm loaf tin with baking paper.

Place the milk, oil, maple syrup, vanilla and mashed pumpkin in a bowl and mix well to combine.

Sift the dry ingredients into a bowl, add the chia seeds and make a well in the centre. Fold in the pumpkin mixture and mix until combined.

Put the nuts and seeds into a bowl, add the spices and mix well.

Spoon half of the pumpkin batter into the prepared tin, top with the spiced nuts and seeds and finish with the remaining batter. Bake for 1½ hours, until a skewer inserted in the bread comes out clean when tested.

Serves 6–8

3 tablespoons milk of your choice

1 tablespoon extra-virgin coconut oil, melted

⅓ cup (80 ml) pure maple syrup

1 teaspoon vanilla powder or natural vanilla extract

2 cups (500 g) mashed roast kent pumpkin (about ½ small pumpkin)

1½ cups (210 g) gluten-free flour

½ cup (90 g) coconut flour

1 teaspoon bicarbonate of soda

1 teaspoon baking powder

½ teaspoon fine sea salt

3 tablespoons chia seeds

1 cup (125 g) walnuts, roughly chopped

2 tablespoons pumpkin seeds, roughly chopped

2 teaspoons ground cinnamon

1 teaspoon ground cardamom

1 teaspoon ground ginger

½ teaspoon freshly grated nutmeg

⅛ teaspoon ground cloves

Haloumi pumpkin omelette

This is a go-to brekkie for me. I eat it out of the pan and it nourishes me completely.

Whisk together the eggs and basil and season with salt and pepper.

Heat the ghee in a 26 cm frypan over a medium–high heat, add the haloumi and cook for 3 minutes each side, until golden brown. Add the tomatoes and kale and cook for 3 minutes or until the tomatoes soften, push them to one side.

Pour the beaten egg into the pan, cook for 3 minutes or until the egg starts to set around the edges, tilting the pan so that any uncooked egg can run underneath.

Add spoonfuls of the roast pumpkin, then cover and cook for 3 minutes or until the top of the omelette is set and the pumpkin is warmed through.

Top with a spoonful of mango chutney, pumpkin seeds and fried shallots.

Serves 1

3 eggs
handful basil leaves, chopped
1 tablespoon ghee
50 g haloumi, sliced thinly
handful cherry tomatoes
handful shredded kale
½ cup roast pumpkin
1 tablespoon mango chutney
1 tablespoon pumpkin seeds
2 tablespoons fried shallots

Pumpkin, tahini and maple smoothie

It's good. Really good. Another great recipe with pumpkin.

Place all ingredients into a high-speed blender. Blend until smooth and creamy.

Serves 2

1 banana
½ teaspoon cinnamon
1 teaspoon chia seeds
1 tablespoon hemp or flax seeds
2 teaspoons hulled tahini
2 tablespoons roasted pumpkin
1 tablespoon psyllium husks
2 teaspoons maple syrup
500 ml almond milk

Ghee-baked fruit

Serve with coconut yoghurt, a warm seed topping or just on their own. Remember, in Ayurveda we don't combine fruit and cow's milk.

Preheat the oven to 160°C.

Halve your chosen fruit and place in a baking dish.

Dot with the ghee, add the spices, sugar and 1 cup of water, then cover and bake.

If using quince, bake for 3 hours, pears approximately 2 hours, mandarins approximately 1 hour and tamarillos around 30 minutes.

Bake until the quince (if using) is pink and the fruit is very soft when tested with a knife.

Serves 4

1.5 kg apples, quinces or pears, mandarins, tamarillos or a combination

3 tablespoons ghee

1 teaspoon fennel seeds

1 cinnamon stick

4 star anise

6 cardamom pods, lightly crushed

3 tablespoons coconut sugar

Eggs with avocado, grains and seeds

Grains are calming and grounding and most are recommended for Vata types. This meal can be eaten warm or at room temperature, and it also makes a lovely warm salad.

Place the rice and quinoa in a rice cooker or saucepan, add 2 cups of water and cook until tender, 12–15 minutes. Remove from the heat and transfer to a bowl. Cover and transfer to the fridge to cool; overnight will give you a crunchier rice.

Heat 2 tablespoons of ghee and the sesame oil in a large frying pan over medium–high heat, add the leek and cook, stirring occasionally, for 5 minutes, until soft. Add the cooked grains, the seeds and tamari and cook, without stirring, for 5 minutes, until heated through and the rice is lightly browned with a little crunch.

Meanwhile, whisk the eggs, push the grain mixture aside in the pan and add the remaining ghee. When the ghee has melted, add the egg to the centre of the pan and gently scramble. Then stir to combine the grains with the egg.

Serve the grains topped with the avocado halves, shredded nori and a sprinkle of the gomasio.

Serves 4

1 cup (200 g) red rice

½ cup (100 g) quinoa, rinsed well

3 tablespoons ghee

1 tablespoon toasted sesame oil

1 leek, white part only, thinly sliced

3 tablespoons pumpkin seeds

3 tablespoons sunflower seeds

3 tablespoons flaxseeds

2 tablespoons tamari

4 eggs

2 avocados, halved

1 nori sheet, finely shredded

3 tablespoons gomasio (toasted sesame seed and salt mix available at health food stores)

Avocado toast 3 ways

Okay, I'm gonna say it, I have no idea why anyone would pay $16 for avocado on toast. Here are a few ideas to give your average avo on toast a run for its money.

MEDITERRANEAN

Smear the feta over the toast, top with the tomato.

Combine the lemon juice, chives and salt in a bowl, add the avocado and gently mix. Spoon on top of the tomato and serve.

2–3 tablespoons marinated goat's feta

4 slices of gluten-free bread, toasted

1–2 tomatoes, sliced

1 tablespoon lemon juice

2 tablespoons snipped chives

1 teaspoon herb salt

1–2 avocados, chopped

CURRIED EGGOCADO WITH SPROUTS

Place the eggs, avocado, curry powder and cashew cheese or mayonnaise in a bowl and roughly mash to combine. Season with salt and pepper. Spread over the toast and top with the sprouts.

3 hard-boiled eggs, peeled

1 avocado, sliced

1 teaspoon mild curry powder

1 tablespoon cashew cheese or mayonnaise

sea salt and freshly ground black pepper

4 slices of gluten-free bread, toasted

a large handful of sprouts of your choice

MISO LOVERS AVOCADO TOAST

Combine the ghee with the miso and spread over the toast.

Top with the avocado, then sprinkle on the nori and toasted black sesame seeds and serve.

Serves 2–4

2 tablespoons ghee, melted

1–2 tablespoons shiro miso

4 slices of gluten-free bread, toasted

1–2 avocados, flesh scooped out of the skin

½ nori sheet, finely shredded

1 tablespoon toasted black sesame seeds

Fragrant vanilla and honey macca cream with berry puree

This is insanely delicious – and so damn simple. Trust me on this one, you won't be sorry. Vanilla powder is expensive but you use so little and the flavour is so vanilla-y that once you have tried it, you'll be won over.

Place the nuts in a bowl, add plenty of water and allow to soak overnight. If you are short on time, you can use boiling water and soak the nuts for 30 minutes, until they are soft.

Place the psyllium husks and 150 ml of water in a bowl. Stir until the mixture thickens and forms a soft gel.

Place the drained soaked nuts in a high-speed blender, add 2 tablespoons of the psyllium gel, the lemon juice, vanilla, half the honey and 1 tablespoon of water and blend until very smooth and creamy. Add a little more water if it is too thick.

To make the berry puree, place the berries and vanilla in a blender and blend until smooth.

Layer the macadamia cream with the berry puree in cups and top with the extra berries and drizzle with the remaining honey.

Serves 4

1½ cups (210 g) macadamia nuts (or cashew nuts)

½ teaspoon psyllium husks

1 teaspoon lemon juice

1 teaspoon vanilla powder

1 tablespoon raw honey

BERRY PUREE

1 cup (125 g) fresh raspberries, plus extra to serve

125 g fresh strawberries, hulled, plus extra to serve

¼ teaspoon vanilla powder

Lunch

Avocado with lentils and nori

Untoasted cold-pressed organic sesame oil is like medicine for Vata types; I recommend it for when you are feeling ungrounded, anxious or just out of sorts.

Divide the spinach between four serving plates. Top with the avocado halves.

Place the lentils, edamame, capsicum, nori and macadamias in a bowl and gently mix to combine.

Divide the lentil mixture between the avocado halves, then spoon some of the remaining mixture onto the spinach leaves.

Whisk together the balsamic vinegar, sesame oil and seeds and drizzle over the avocado and spinach leaves.

Serves 4

2 large handfuls of snow pea tendrils or baby spinach leaves

2 avocados, halved and peeled

1 cup (200 g) cooked puy lentils

½ cup (65 g) cooked shelled edamame

½ red capsicum, finely chopped

1 nori sheet, roughly torn

¼ cup (40 g) roughly chopped macadamia nuts

DRESSING

2 tablespoons balsamic vinegar

1 tablespoon toasted sesame oil

2 tablespoons organic sesame seeds

Roasted whole sweet potato topped with herbed dhal

Soak the dhal in cold water overnight; drain well.

Preheat the oven to 180°C. Line a baking tray with baking paper.

Place the sweet potato, capsicum and onion on the lined tray. Roast for 45 minutes, until the sweet potato is very soft and starting to release its sugars.

While the vegetables are roasting, place the dhal in a saucepan, add 3 cups of water, the coconut oil, garam masala, mustard seeds and tamarind puree and bring to the boil. Reduce the heat to low and simmer for 30 minutes, until the dhal is soft and creamy. Remove from the heat and stir through the herbs.

Cut each sweet potato in half lengthways, top with the herbed dhal and finish with the roast capsicum and onion. Serve with a dollop of yoghurt.

Serves 4

NOTE: *Chana dhal (also known as bengal gram) are hulled and split black chickpeas. They are available from wholefood stores and Indian grocers.*

1 cup (210 g) chana dhal or whole mung dhal (see Note)

4 small sweet potatoes (about 800 g), unpeeled

1 red capsicum, thinly sliced

1 red onion, thinly sliced

1 tablespoon extra-virgin coconut oil

1 teaspoon garam masala

½ teaspoon black mustard seeds

1 tablespoon tamarind puree

2 tablespoons chopped coriander

2 tablespoons chopped mint

½ cup (125 g) coconut yoghurt

Sweet corn with popped quinoa and green pepper gomasio

This recipe is inspired from a trip I took to Mexico for my 50th birthday. Street corners were filled with vendors selling chargrilled corn topped with finely grated queso (Mexican cheese) and a pinch of locally smoked pepper.

Cook the corn until soft and sweet. Depending on the time of year, you may want to cook it on the barbecue or on top of the stove in a saucepan of boiling water.

Place the quinoa in a frying pan and cook over medium heat until it starts to pop in the pan, about 3 minutes.

Combine the quinoa, sesame seeds, pumpkin seeds, peppercorns, paprika, salt and parmesan in a shallow bowl or tray large enough to hold the corn and mix well.

Roll the corn in the ghee, then in the quinoa, parmesan green pepper mix and serve.

Serves 4

4 corn cobs

1 tablespoon tricolour quinoa, rinsed and patted dry

3 tablespoons sesame seeds, toasted

1 tablespoon roughly chopped pumpkin seeds

1 tablespoon fresh or dried green peppercorns, coarsely crushed

1 teaspoon smoked or sweet paprika

sea salt

½ cup (50 g) finely grated parmesan

3 tablespoons ghee

Roast vegetable salad with coriander seed puree

I favour roasted veg on cooler days, steamed veg in spring and summer and raw veg on very hot days. This salad is the bomb, the coriander puree is something I am pretty sure you will put on everything.

Preheat the oven to 200°C. Line two large baking trays with baking paper.

Arrange the vegetables and tempeh or tofu on the prepared tray, drizzle with the olive oil and sprinkle on some salt. Roast for 40 minutes to 1 hour until all the vegetables are soft. Some may cook more quickly than others, so take them out when they are ready.

Meanwhile, to make the coriander seed puree, place the herbs, garlic, lime juice, chilli, yoghurt and seeds in a blender and blend until smooth.

Spoon the coriander seed puree onto a large serving plate, pile the roasted vegetables and tempeh or tofu on top.

Serves 4

2 red capsicum, cut into thick strips

2 fennel bulbs, sliced

2 red onion, cut into wedges

2 carrots, cut into thick rounds

500 g sweet potato, unpeeled, cut into thick wedges

3 zucchinis, cut lengthways into thick slices

300 g tempeh or tofu, cut into thick batons

3 tablespoons olive oil

sea salt

CORIANDER SEED PUREE

2 cups (40 g) coriander and mint leaves

1 garlic clove, crushed

1½ tablespoons lime juice

1 green chilli, chopped

1 cup (250 g) coconut yoghurt

3 tablespoons roughly chopped pumpkin seeds

Poke bowl

I am a big fan of fresh fish but am in an ethical dilemma about the unsustainable catches we are pulling from the oceans. I avoid eating tuna because I feel it is overfished and instead eat only local fish. A firm boneless fish is what you need for poke. I've made it with snapper, marlin, kingfish, salmon and, my favourite, mackerel.

To make the poke, place the fish, sesame oil, tamari, rice vinegar, spring onion and sesame seeds in a bowl and mix to combine. Cover and allow to marinate in the refrigerator for 4 hours, or overnight if time permits.

Dry roast the rice in a frying pan over medium heat for 3–5 minutes, until it is golden brown. Transfer to a saucepan or rice cooker, add 4 cups of water and bring to the boil. Reduce the heat, cover and cook for 25 minutes, until the rice is soft.

Add the carrot and seaweed to the fish poke and mix to combine.

Divide the rice between serving bowls, then top with the poke, avocado, edamame, pickled ginger and kimchi (if using) and a good squeeze of lime.

Serves 4

500 g fish of your choice (such as kingfish, snapper, mackerel), cut into 2 cm cubes

1 teaspoon toasted sesame oil

2 tablespoons tamari

2 teaspoons rice vinegar

2 spring onions, thinly sliced

1 tablespoon black sesame seeds

2 cups (400 g) long-grain brown rice

2 carrots, finely shredded

1 cup (150 g) seaweed salad

1 avocado, chopped

2 cups (260 g) cooked shelled edamame

3 tablespoons pickled ginger

½ cup (125 g) kimchi (optional)

lime wedges, to serve

Chicken chilli ramen

Because Vata types can have fragile tummies, I recommend you use gluten-free pure buckwheat noodles.

Put the chicken into a shallow non-metallic bowl, add the chilli flakes, tamari, sake, mirin and sugar and mix to coat the chicken. Cover and marinate in the fridge for 30 minutes, or longer if time permits.

Heat your barbecue to hot or a chargrill pan over medium–high heat. Drain the chicken and pat dry. Lightly oil the barbecue or pan and cook the chicken on all sides until golden brown and tender, about 7–10 minutes. Allow to stand in a warm place for 10 minutes before cutting into thick slices.

Meanwhile, cook the noodles in a large pan of boiling water until tender, and drain well. Divide the noodles between four serving bowls.

Gently heat the miso ramen broth until it is just about to boil. Immediately ladle over the noodles. Top with the chicken, corn, egg, spinach and pickled ginger.

Serves 4

4 chicken thigh fillets, skin off

½ teaspoon chilli flakes

1 tablespoon tamari

1 tablespoon sake

1 tablespoon mirin

1 teaspoon caster sugar

1 tablespoon sunflower oil

200 g dried buckwheat or ramen noodles

4 cups (1 litre) Miso Ramen Broth (page 219)

200 g corn kernels

2 hard-boiled eggs, peeled and halved

2 handfuls of baby spinach leaves

2 tablespoons pickled ginger

Saffron, fennel, pea and asparagus risotto

Rice is great medicine for Vata types and should be something they regularly include in their diet. This recipe takes advantage of spring vegetables but you could substitute for sweet potato or pumpkin if you like.

Place the stock, wine and saffron in a saucepan, bring to the boil, reduce the heat and hold at a low simmer.

Heat the oil in a large frying pan, add the onion and cook, stirring occasionally, over medium heat for 10 minutes, until the onion is soft but not browned.

Add the garlic, fennel seeds and fennel to the pan and cook for 5–7 minutes, until the fennel starts to soften and turn golden. Stir in the rice and cook, stirring, for 2 minutes, until the rice is coated in the oil.

Add 1 cup of simmering stock to the pan, stirring until the liquid is absorbed. Once it has been absorbed, add another cup, then continue stirring and adding stock until all the stock has been used and the rice is soft, about 20 minutes. You want a soupy creamy risotto.

Add the asparagus, peas, ghee or butter and parmesan and cook for a further 5 minutes. Season and serve.

Serves 4

4 cups (1 litre) homemade Vegetable or Chicken Stock (pages 220 and 224)
1 cup (250 ml) white wine
pinch of saffron threads
3 tablespoons olive oil
1 onion, chopped
1 garlic clove, chopped
1 teaspoon fennel seeds
1 small fennel bulb, thinly sliced
300 g risotto rice
1 bunch of asparagus, woody ends trimmed, chopped
1 cup (130 g) frozen baby peas
3 tablespoons ghee or butter
½ cup (150 g) finely grated parmesan cheese
sea salt and freshly ground black pepper

Japanese pumpkin, carrot and daikon

You need to slow simmer this dish, and the flavour is always better the next day. Perfect with some brown rice.

Roughly peel the pumpkin, leaving on several patches of skin. Discard the seeds and cut the flesh into large bite-sized pieces.

Place the pumpkin, daikon, carrot and lotus root (if using) in a large saucepan, add 2 cups of water, the sake, mirin and tamari and bring to the boil. Reduce the heat to low, cover and cook for 40 minutes, until the pumpkin is soft.

Sprinkle the black sesame seeds and coriander over the top and serve with brown rice.

Serves 4

NOTE: *Lotus root is the root of the water lotus flower. It can be purchased fresh or frozen in Asian food stores. The flavour is bland so potato could be used instead.*

750 g green-skinned pumpkin (like kent)
1 daikon, scrubbed and cut into thick half moons
1 carrot, peeled and cut into thick half moons
1 lotus root, sliced (see Note) (optional)
1 tablespoon sake
1 tablespoon mirin
1 tablespoon tamari

To serve
1 tablespoon black sesame seeds
coriander sprigs
steamed brown rice

Pumpkin 3 ways

ROAST PUMPKIN

Preheat your oven to 200°C. Place the pumpkin on a baking tray and roast for 1 hour. Cut in half and scoop out seeds.

1 kent or butternut pumpkin (something sweet and creamy)

NOURISHING PUMPKIN SOUP

Heat the oil in a large saucepan, add the leek and onion and cook, stirring occasionally, over medium heat for 10 minutes, until the onion and leek are soft.

Add the cinnamon, bay leaf, pumpkin, mung dhal, stock, nutritional yeast and nutmeg and bring to the boil. Reduce the heat and simmer, covered, for 20 minutes.

Blend and top with sesame seeds and furikake.

Serves 4

1 roast pumpkin (flesh only, see above)

2 tablespoons olive oil

1 leek, white part only, thinly sliced

1 onion, chopped

1 cinnamon stick

1 bay leaf

¼ cup (60 g) split mung dhal

4 cups (1 litre) Vegetable or Chicken Stock (pages 220 and 224)

1 tablespoon nutritional yeast

½ teaspoon freshly grated nutmeg

2 tablespoons black sesame seeds, toasted

1 tablespoon furikake

WARM PUMPKIN SALAD WITH YOGHURT, SEEDS AND SRIRACHA

Cut top off roast pumpkin. Remove seeds. Top with dollops of yoghurt and scatter over the leaves, pumpkin seeds, raisins and drizzle with sriracha and olive oil.

Serves 4

1 roast pumpkin

½ cup (125 ml) Greek-style yoghurt or labneh

2 handfuls of mixed leaves

2 tablespoons pumpkin seeds

2 tablespoons raisins

1 tablespoon sriracha chilli sauce

2 tablespoons olive oil

PUMPKIN PORRIDGE

Place the grain, pumpkin, spices and milk in a pan and cook, stirring, over medium heat until heated through. Serve with the black tahini, coconut cream and maple syrup.

Serves 1–2

1 cup (185 g) cooked grain

½ cup mashed roast pumpkin

1 teaspoon each ground turmeric, ginger, cinnamon

½ teaspoon ground cardamom

1 cup (250 ml) almond milk

black tahini, coconut cream and maple syrup to serve

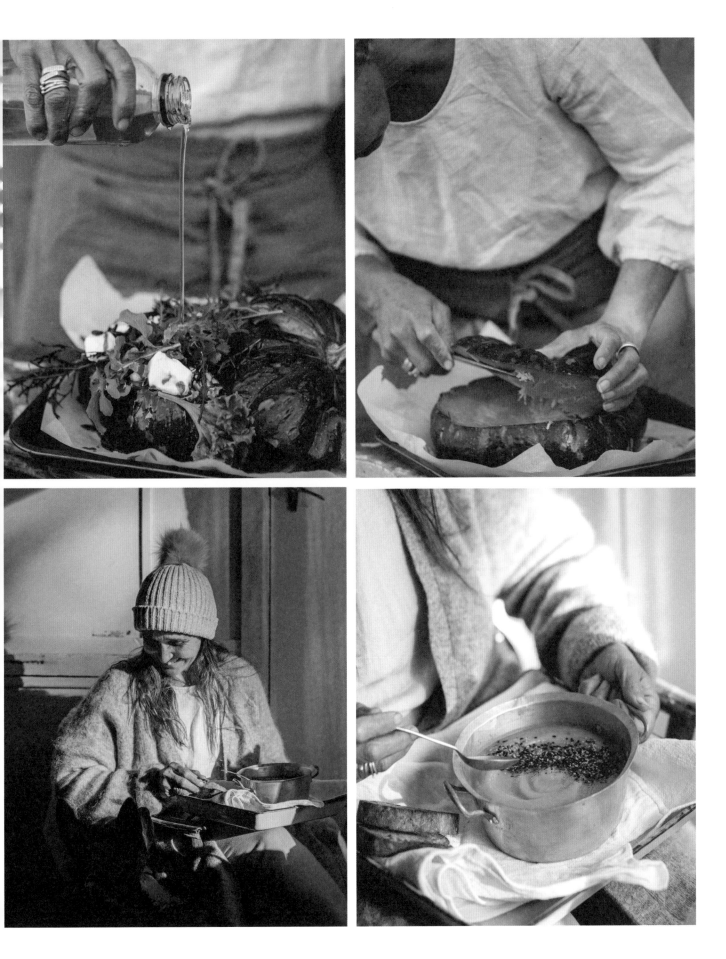

Chopped egg, artichoke and olive salad

This is a simple throw-together or should I say chop-together salad. Make sure you have a big chopping board for this one and then you can serve it to guests on the board.

Using a very large chopping board, slice the spring onions, add the cucumber and chop together with the spring onion. Add the lettuce and shred, then fold the salad ingredients into each other.

Add the snow pea tendrils or sprouts, olives, artichokes, goat's cheese, avocado, eggs and chop until all the ingredients are combined.

Make a space in the middle of the salad and add the dressing ingredients. Mix the mustard, lemon juice, oregano and olive oil together, then fold the dressing into the chopped salad.

Serves 4

3 spring onions, trimmed

1 Lebanese cucumber
(about 150 g), trimmed

150 g mixed salad leaves

100 g snow pea tendrils or sprouts

1 cup (150 g) pitted kalamata olives

100 g marinated artichokes, drained

100 g goat's cheese

1 avocado, stone removed and peeled

2 hard boiled eggs, peeled

DRESSING

1 tablespoon dijon mustard

1 tablespoon lemon juice

1 teaspoon dried oregano

2 tablespoons extra-virgin olive oil

Dinner

Our digestive system slows down after 2 pm and a lot of Vata types struggle with annoying gut issues at this time of day; going to bed with a full tummy will not help, so I encourage you to eat your largest meal in the middle of the day or enjoy an early dinner.

In winter, a broth or soup is the perfect choice for dinner; in summer it can be a salad or some steamed vegetables. Try to avoid skipping dinner, as Vata is affected by the elements of air and space, and the more space you leave between meals, the more tummy problems you may have.

Aim to create a relaxed atmosphere and limit your conversation during your meal. Vata types love a good chat but talking too much when you are eating can impact on your delicate digestive system.

Baked celeriac and fennel soup

If you have not tried celeriac before, it tastes like a mixture of celery and parsnip. This really simple recipe may take some time but I find baking is the best way to cook celeriac. You can just roast the whole celeriac and eat it as you would a baked potato.

Preheat the oven to 150°C.

Scrub the celeriac bulb to remove any dirt and rub with the ghee or olive oil.

Place the fennel seeds, salt and pepper in a mortar and pestle and crush to a coarse powder. Sprinkle generously over the celeriac, then wrap it in foil. Bake for 2 hours until the flesh is very soft, think baked potato consistency. Slice the baby fennel and place into a baking dish and drizzle with a little olive oil and sprinkle with some of the fennel salt. Check after 1 hour and if the baby fennel is ready, remove it from the pan and set aside.

Split the celeriac in half or quarters and finish with a generous spoonful of ghee or butter and a sprinkle of parsley, nutritional yeast and paprika.

If you choose to make a soup, add the baked celeriac flesh to a pan, add the chicken stock and bring to the boil, reduce heat and simmer for 10 minutes, stirring several times to prevent it catching on the bottom of the pan. Blend until smooth. Serve topped with roasted baby fennel and drizzled with sesame oil.

Serves 4

1 celeriac bulb (about 500 g)
3 bulbs baby fennel (about 400 g)
2 tablespoons ghee or olive oil
1 teaspoon fennel seeds
sea salt and freshly ground black pepper
1.5 litre chicken stock

To serve
ghee or butter
finely chopped flat-leaf parsley
nutritional yeast
sweet paprika

Roast miso chicken

Here is my version of roast chicken. It is truly delicious. I use a light-coloured miso and if you can pop the miso mixture under the skin then leave the chicken on a rack in the fridge for an hour or so this will give you a lovely crisp skin.

Preheat the oven to 200°C.

Rinse the chicken under cold water; pat dry inside and out with paper towel. Place the ghee, miso, mirin and tamari into a bowl and mix until it is smooth. Gently lift and slide your hand under the breast skin to separate the skin from the flesh, then carefully rub the ghee mixture between the skin and flesh. Rub the chicken skin all over with the remaining ghee.

Put the halved baby leek and garlic into a large roasting tin. Place the chicken on the bed of leeks. Roast for 15 minutes. Reduce the oven temperature to 180°C and continue to roast the chicken for 1 hour until the juices run clear when you test the thickest part of the thigh. Remove the chicken and place on a plate, cover with foil and allow to rest for 10 minutes before you carve it. The juices from the chicken will be in the bottom of the pan and can be used to pour over the sliced chicken.

Carve the chicken and serve with the baby leeks and your choice of vegetables.

Serves 4

1.6 kg chicken

3 tablespoons ghee, melted

1 heaped tablespoon shiro miso and light miso

2 tablespoons mirin

1 tablespoon tamari

1 tablespoon ghee, for basting skin

6 baby leeks, halved

1 head garlic, halved

Flash-fried greens with lemon

Heat the ghee in a wok or large deep frypan over medium–high heat, add the broccoli and a good splash of water and stir-fry for 5 minutes until the broccoli is bright green and softened.

Add the edamame, peas and snow peas and stir-fry for 2 minutes or until tender.

Remove the pan from the heat, add the lemon juice and zest and season with salt and pepper.

Serves 4 as a side

3 tablespoons ghee

300 g broccoli, cut into long thin wedges

1 cup (130 g) shelled edamame

1 cup (130 g) peas

200 g snow peas, trimmed

zest and juice of 2 lemons

Steamed vegetable bowl with lemony tofu cream

Fabulous for a meat-free meal, this tofu cream is simple to whip up. Just make sure you soak the cashews, as this makes the nuts more digestible and the cream more creamy.

Place the brussels sprouts, corn and sweet potato in a steamer basket or large colander over a saucepan of simmering water. Cover and cook for 20 minutes, until just soft. Add the broccoli and edamame and steam for a further 5 minutes, until tender and bright green.

While the vegetables are cooking, make the tofu cream. Drain the cashews. Place the cashews and tofu in a food processor, add the garlic, lemon juice, mustard and nutritional yeast and process until smooth and creamy.

Serve the vegetables with the tofu cream on the side.

Serves 4

300 g brussels sprouts

4 small corn cobs

300 g white sweet potato, cut into thick slices

300 g broccoli, cut into florets

200 g frozen shelled edamame

TOFU CREAM

1 cup (155 g) raw cashews, soaked in cold water for 2 hours

250 g silken tofu

2 small garlic cloves, peeled

2 tablespoons lemon juice

2 tablespoons dijon mustard

2 tablespoons nutritional yeast

Pumpkin ricotta slice with lemony greens

This is a beautiful meal to serve up to vegetarians and, if you have roast pumpkin on hand, it is simple and really quick to put together. It can also be made ahead and reheated. Try to buy good-quality fresh ricotta.

Preheat the oven to 180°C. Line a 20 cm x 30 cm baking dish with baking paper.

Place the pumpkin in a large bowl.

Roughly mash the ricotta in another bowl, then add to the pumpkin with the lemon zest, thyme, nutmeg, flour, eggs and salt and pepper.

Spread the mixture in the prepared dish and bake for 40 minutes, until firm. Allow to stand for 10 minutes before slicing into tiles.

Meanwhile, for the lemony greens, steam the kale and silverbeet in a steamer or colander set over a saucepan of simmering water until bright green and tender, about 5 minutes. Add the lemon juice and olive oil and toss to combine.

Melt the ghee in a small frying pan over medium heat, add the pine nuts and cook, stirring occasionally, for 3 minutes, until the pine nuts are golden.

Serve the pumpkin tiles on a bed of steamed lemony greens finished with the ghee and pine nuts.

Serves 4

3 cups (750 g) roast pumpkin (page 86)

250 g fresh ricotta

zest of 1 lemon

1 tablespoon roughly chopped lemon thyme

pinch of freshly grated nutmeg

2 cups (280 g) gluten-free flour

3 eggs, lightly beaten

sea salt and freshly ground black pepper

3 tablespoons ghee

3 tablespoons pine nuts

LEMONY GREENS

1 bunch of kale (about 400 g), central stems removed, leaves roughly chopped

2 cups (260 g) roughly chopped silverbeet

juice of 1–2 lemons, depending on how lemony you like it

1 tablespoon extra-virgin olive oil

Urad dhal makhani

Urad dhal are small oval-shaped black beans (not the same as black turtle beans or black beluga lentils) and are available in Indian stores.

Soak the urad dhal overnight in cold water. Rinse and drain well.

Place the dhal in a saucepan, add 3 cups of water and bring to the boil. Reduce the heat to low and cook for 1 hour until the dhal is very soft and most of the water has evaporated.

Melt 2 tablespoons of ghee in a large saucepan, add the cumin seeds, chilli, cloves and cardamom and cook over medium heat for 2 minutes, until fragrant. Add the chilli powder, turmeric, ginger and tomatoes and bring to the boil. Reduce the heat and simmer for 15 minutes.

Add the dhal to the pan and simmer for a further 15 minutes, until thick and creamy. If the mixture is too thick, add ½ cup water and warm through. Remove from the heat, stir in the extra ghee and season with salt. Serve as a light meal with some steamed rice.

Serves 4

1 cup (210 g) urad dhal or whole mung dhal

2 tablespoons ghee, plus 3 tablespoons extra to serve

1 teaspoon cumin seeds

1 small green chilli, split down the middle

2 cloves

3 green cardamom pods, lightly crushed

½ teaspoon chilli powder

½ teaspoon ground turmeric

½ teaspoon ground ginger

1 x 400 g can diced tomatoes

sea salt

steamed rice, to serve

Mild green curry with eggs and cashews

Heat the oil in a wok or large saucepan, add the onion and cook over medium heat for 5 minutes, until it starts to soften. Stir in the ginger and garlic and cook until fragrant. Add the curry paste and 2 tablespoons of the thick coconut cream from the top of the can. Cook for 3 minutes, until the oil starts to separate from the curry paste.

Add the carrot, capsicums, zucchini and broccoli stems and pour in the remaining coconut cream. Add the cashews, sunflowers seeds, kaffir lime leaves, fish sauce or lime juice and 1 cup of water and bring to the boil, reduce the heat and simmer for 20 minutes.

Add the eggs, broccoli florets and snow peas and cook for 5 minutes, until the broccoli is tender. Serve with rice.

Serves 4

2 tablespoons extra-virgin coconut oil

1 red onion, chopped

1 tablespoon grated ginger

1 large garlic clove, grated

2 tablespoons mild green curry paste

1 x 400 ml can coconut cream

2 carrots, cut into thick slices

1 small red capsicum, roughly chopped

1 small green capsicum, roughly chopped

1 zucchini, sliced

200 g broccoli, stem sliced and cut into florets

a handful of raw cashews

2 tablespoons sunflower seeds

8 kaffir lime leaves

1 tablespoon fish sauce or lime juice

4 hard-boiled eggs, peeled

100 g snow peas, trimmed

steamed rice, to serve

Vegetable lasagne

I've been making veg lasagne for as long as I can remember – I love that I can pack so many vegetables into one dish and don't think I've ever made it the same way twice. Yes, I know it takes a while to make but it is seriously worth it. I roast loads of vegetables at the beginning of the week and have them waiting in the fridge ready to prepare salads and meals like this.

I find people struggle with making white sauce, so I've ditched it in this recipe and gone for a cauliflower and ricotta combo instead.

Preheat the oven to 200°C. Line two large baking trays with baking paper.

Arrange the pumpkin, capsicum, zucchini and garlic on the prepared trays, drizzle with 2 tablespoons of olive oil and sprinkle with the salt. Roast the smaller vegetables for 40 minutes and the pumpkin for 1 hour until all the vegetables are soft. Cut the pumpkin into thick wedges. Peel and mash the garlic.

While the vegetables are roasting, heat the remaining oil in a large, deep frying pan, add the onion and cook, stirring occasionally, over medium heat for 10 minutes, until soft. Add the roasted garlic, tomatoes and vinegar and bring to the boil. Reduce the heat and cook for 25 minutes, until reduced by one-third. You want to have some moisture left in the sauce as this will help to cook the lasagne sheets. Stir in the basil leaves and olives and season with salt and pepper.

Combine the ricotta, cauliflower and milk in a bowl and season well with salt and pepper.

Spoon a little of the tomato sauce into the base of a 20 cm x 30 cm lasagne dish (this stops the lasagne sheets from sticking to the bottom of the dish). Cover with a layer of lasagne sheets, spoon over half the tomato sauce, then add half the capsicum and zucchini, top with another layer of lasagne sheets, half the spinach, half the pumpkin and half the ricotta mixture and sprinkle with half the parmesan. Continue layering, finishing with the ricotta mixture and parmesan.

Bake the lasagne for 50 minutes, until the lasagne sheets are soft and the topping is golden brown. Allow to stand for 10 minutes before slicing.

Serves 6–8

¼ kent pumpkin (about 1 kg)

2 red capsicums, cut into thick slices

3 zucchini, cut lengthways into long thick slices

1 head of garlic

3 tablespoons olive oil

sea salt

1 onion, chopped

2 x 400 g cans diced tomatoes

1 tablespoon balsamic vinegar

a handful of basil leaves, torn

⅓ cup (50 g) pitted roughly chopped kalamata olives

freshly ground black pepper

500 g fresh ricotta

1 cup (100 g) grated cauliflower

1 cup (250 ml) milk of your choice

350 g gluten-free lasagne sheets

500 g English spinach or baby spinach leaves, trimmed

1 cup (135 g) finely grated parmesan

Ghee 3 ways

The recipe for ghee can be found in the Food Medicine section, page 213.

GHEE INFUSED WITH VATA-CALMING SPICES WITH BASMATI RICE

Place the ghee, spices and salt into a small frypan over a medium heat, and cook for 3 minutes or until the spices are fragrant. Pour over the cooked basmati rice.

Serves 4

- 3 tablespoons ghee
- 1 teaspoon ground turmeric
- 1 teaspoon cumin seeds
- 1 teaspoon ground coriander
- 1 teaspoon fennel seeds
- pinch of salt
- 2 cups cooked basmati rice

GHEE SWEET SMOKY MAPLE NUTS AND SEEDS

Serve on salads, breakfast cereals or with baked fruit.

Place the ghee, nuts, seeds, spices and salt into a frypan and cook for 5-10 minutes until the nuts are fragrant and golden. Add the maple syrup and cook for 2 minutes. Remove and serve at once or allow to cool, then store in an airtight container for up to 2 weeks.

Serves 4

- 2 tablespoons ghee
- 1 cup (140 g) mixed raw nuts
- 1 cup (150 g) mixed seeds (pumpkin, sunflower, flax, hemp)
- 1 teaspoon ground cinnamon
- 1 teaspoon ground cardamom
- 1 teaspoon fennel seeds
- pinch of smoked salt
- 1–2 tablespoons pure maple syrup

ANXIETY CALMING MILKY GHEE DRINK

Place the milk, spices, ghee and dates into a pan and heat gently until it is about to come to a boil.

Remove from heat and allow to stand for 5 minutes to infuse.

Serves 2

- 2 cups (500 ml) unhomogenised organic milk
- 1 teaspoon cinnamon
- 1 teaspoon cardamom
- ½ teaspoon ground ginger
- pinch saffron
- pinch pepper
- 1 teaspoon ghee
- 2 medjool dates, seeds removed, finely chopped

Sweet treats, snacks and drinks

Black sesame spice crackers

Crackers are not something Vata types should eat a lot of because they are crisp and dry. So I've created these warming Vata-friendly crackers using black tahini for you. I have used black tahini, as it is particularly grounding and good Vata medicine – and I love it – and cumin and fennel seeds, as they are great digestive spices.

Preheat the oven to 170°C. Line a baking tray with baking paper.

Place the tahini, egg, seeds, nutritional yeast, salt and almond meal in a bowl and mix to combine.

Gather the tahini mixture into a ball, then flatten slightly. Roll out between two sheets of baking paper to 1 cm thick. Peel off the top layer of paper, sprinkle on fennel and cumin seeds, pressing in gently, and mark the dough rectangles to make cutting easier after it is baked.

Transfer the dough to the lined tray and bake for 15 minutes, until crisp and golden. Don't be concerned: the oil will foam to the surface as the cracker cooks but it will settle as the cracker cools. Allow to cool on the tray before breaking into crackers. Store in an airtight container for up to 1 week.

Serves 4

3 tablespoons black or hulled tahini

1 egg, lightly beaten

3 tablespoons mixed seeds (such as sesame, pumpkin, sunflower, flax, hemp)

1 tablespoon nutritional yeast

a generous pinch of sea salt

½ cup (55 g) almond meal

1 teaspoon fennel seeds

1 teaspoon cumin seeds

Smoked fish and cashew paste

One of my favourite recipes in this book. So simple. So damn tasty.

Place the cashews in a bowl, cover with water and allow to soak overnight; drain well.

Transfer the cashews to a food processor, add the smoked fish, lemon zest and juice, nutritional yeast and olive oil and process until smooth. Transfer to a bowl, stir in the chives and mix well to combine.

Serve this paste with the toast smeared with ghee.

Serves 4

½ cup (80 g) raw cashews

150 g smoked fish (I use rainbow trout), flaked

zest of 1 lemon

1 tablespoon lemon juice

2 teaspoons nutritional yeast

2 tablespoons olive oil

2 tablespoons snipped chives

To serve
slices of sourdough bread, toasted
ghee

Roasted sweet potato chips

These make a great snack or side. I add them to nourish bowls or serve them as a nibble for guests. You can change the seasoning; often I throw in a pinch of chilli to warm things up.

Preheat the oven to 200°C. Line a baking tray with baking paper.

Place the sweet potato in a bowl, add the coconut oil and salt and toss to coat. Spread the potato in a single layer over the lined tray and bake for 45 minutes, until crisp and cooked through.

Makes 2 cups

500 g sweet potato, scrubbed and cut into wedges
1 tablespoon extra-virgin coconut oil, melted
1 tablespoon herbed vegetable salt

Almonds, raisins and seeds with vanilla and orange

In Ayurveda, we soak nuts before eating them to help them become more digestible. Soaking almonds and raisins is often prescribed for those who have issues with constipation.

Place the almonds, raisins, seeds, zest and juice, spices and vanilla in a bowl, cover with 3 tablespoons of water and allow to soak overnight. Drain and enjoy as a snack. Store in an airtight container in the refrigerator for up to 2 days.

Makes 1 cup

a handful of almonds
a handful of raisins
seeds of your choice
zest and juice of 1 orange or mandarin
3 cardamom pods, lightly crushed
1 teaspoon fennel seeds, lightly bruised
1 teaspoon vanilla powder or natural vanilla extract

Best ever carrot cake

I am a firm believer that all birthdays must be celebrated with cake. I have a few tried-and-tested recipes that I make over and over, and this is a firm favourite.

Preheat the oven to 180°C. Grease and line a 22cm springform cake tin with baking paper.

Place the eggs and sugar in a large bowl and beat until pale and thick. Add the vanilla and oil and beat until combined. Fold in the carrot, dates, flour, almond meal, baking powder, bicarbonate of soda, spices and nuts. Spoon into the prepared tin and smooth the top.

Bake the cake for 50–55 minutes, until a skewer inserted in the centre comes out clean. Set aside to cool in the tin.

To make the icing, beat the ghee, cream cheese and maple syrup until light and creamy.

Using a serrated knife, cut the cake in half crossways to create two layers. Spread the top of one layer with half the icing. Top with the other layer and finish with the remaining icing. Decorate as desired and serve.

Serves 8

4 eggs

½ cup (125 g) coconut sugar

1 teaspoon vanilla powder or natural vanilla extract

250 ml ghee or olive oil

4 carrots, grated

6 medjool dates, stones removed, flesh finely chopped

2 cups (250 g) gluten-free flour (I use a brown rice and arrowroot combination)

½ cup (125 g) almond meal

1 teaspoon baking powder

1 teaspoon bicarbonate of soda

2 teaspoons ground cinnamon

1 teaspoon ground cardamom

120 g roasted hazelnuts, chopped

ICING

125 g ghee, softened

250 g cream cheese, softened and chopped

3 tablespoons pure maple syrup

Honey and orange blossom tahini whip

I'm a big tahini fan and as I've mentioned earlier it is great Vata medicine, as it's oily and calming. Store tahini at room temperature out of direct sunlight as it is high in oil and can turn rancid; if you put it in the fridge it goes as hard as a rock and is a nightmare to work with.

Place the tahini, cinnamon, honey, vanilla, orange blossom water (if using), orange zest and 2 tablespoons of water in a bowl and mix until smooth and well combined.

Transfer the tahini whip to a serving bowl and top with the chopped pistachios. Serve with the berries and figs for dipping.

Serves 4

½ cup (140 g) hulled tahini, at room temperature

1 teaspoon ground cinnamon

1 teaspoon raw honey

1 teaspoon vanilla powder or natural vanilla extract

1 teaspoon orange blossom water (optional)

2 teaspoons grated orange zest

1 tablespoon chopped unsalted pistachio kernels

200 g mixed fresh strawberries, raspberries and/or blueberries

4 figs

Coconut jam cake

Preheat the oven to 180°C. Grease and line the base and sides of a 20 cm x 10 cm loaf tin with baking paper.

Place the almond meal, coconut and coconut sugar into a bowl and mix to combine.

Whisk together the vanilla extract, eggs, melted coconut oil, rosemary, rosewater, lemon zest and juice.

Add the wet ingredients to the dry ingredients and mix to combine.

Spoon half the mixture into the prepared tin. Drop teaspoons of the jam over the surface of the mixture, top with the remaining mixture. Bake for 30 minutes or until a skewer comes out clean when inserted into the centre.

Makes 1 loaf

150 g (1⅓ cups) almond meal

1 cup (100 g) desiccated coconut

⅔ cup (140 g) coconut sugar

1 teaspoon vanilla extract

4 eggs

200 g coconut oil, melted

1 tablespoon finely chopped rosemary

1 tablespoon rosewater

zest and juice 1 lemon

2 tablespoons berry jam

Mulled Vata tea

Place the teabags, sugar, orange zest and juice, cloves, cinnamon, vanilla and star anise into a saucepan. Add 3 cups (750 ml) boiling water and bring to a boil then reduce heat and simmer for 5 minutes.

Strain and serve with extra orange rind.

2 rooibos tea bags

1 tablespoon coconut sugar

zest and juice 1 orange

2 cloves

1 cinnamon stick

1 vanilla pod, halved

1 star anise

orange rind to serve

Black sesame 3 ways

BLACK SESAME, SALT AND CHOC CHUNK COOKIES

Preheat the oven to 180°C. Line a large baking tray with baking paper.

Place the tahini, sugar and egg in a bowl and mix until mixture comes away from the side of the bowl and forms a ball similar to a dough consistency.

Shape tablespoons of the tahini mixture into balls, place on the prepared tray and flatten slightly. Top with the chopped chocolate and sprinkle with a little salt. Bake for 10–12 minutes.

Makes 12

1 cup (250 g) black tahini
⅔ cup (160 g) coconut sugar
1 egg, lightly beaten
100 g dark chocolate, roughly chopped
rough sea salt

BLACK SESAME PORRIDGE

Rinse and drain the oats and place in a pan with the black tahini, salt and milk and bring to boil. Reduce heat and simmer for 10 minutes or until the oats are soft.

Stir in the sugar and ginger to combine.

Serve bowls of the porridge topped with the goji, seeds and ghee.

Serves 4

1 cup steel cut oats (160 g), soaked overnight in cold water
2 tablespoons black tahini
pinch sea salt
1½ cups (375 ml) unhomogenised organic milk or coconut milk
2 teaspoons coconut sugar
1 teaspoon finely sliced ginger

To serve
2 tablespoons goji berries
1 teaspoon black sesame seeds
2 tablespoons pumpkin seeds
3 tablespoons pomegranate seeds
1 tablespoon ghee

BLACK SESAME GREENS

Steam the greens in a steamer or colander set over a saucepan of simmering water until bright green and tender, about 5 minutes.

Place the tahini, sesame seeds, tamari, sesame oil and ½ cup of water in a small saucepan and cook, stirring, until warmed through. If the mixture is too thick, add more water. You want it to be a pouring consistency.

Pour the black sesame mixture over the vegetables and gently toss to combine.

1 bunch of broccolini
300 g green beans, trimmed
1 cup (200 g) frozen shelled edamame or baby peas
2 tablespoons black tahini
2 tablespoons black sesame seeds
2 tablespoons tamari
2 teaspoons organic sesame oil

GODDESS DIVINE ENERGY

Vegan Choc Peanut Butter Cake

Yes it's good. Really, really good.

Preheat oven to 180°C. Grease and line a heart-shaped cake tin or 22cm springform tin with baking paper.

Place the almond meal, coconut, coconut sugar, cacao, buckwheat flour, baking powder and chia seeds into a bowl and stir to combine.

Combine the peanut butter, banana and coconut water, then fold into the dry ingredients.

Spoon the mixture into the prepared tin and bake for 40–50 minutes or until a skewer comes out mostly clean when inserted in the centre. (It will be slightly moist because of the nature of the cake.)

Allow to cool for 10 minutes in the tin before turning out onto a wire rack to cool completely.

To make the topping, place the banana, cacao, maple syrup and tahini into a food processor and process until smooth and creamy.

Spread over the cooled cake, top with the flaked coconut and drizzle with the maple syrup.

Serves 8

1 cup (100 g) almond meal

1 cup (100 g) dessicated coconut

½ cup (125 g) coconut sugar

½ cup (85 g) cacao powder

3 tablespoons buckwheat flour

2 teaspoons baking powder

2 tablespoons chia seeds

2 teaspoons peanut butter or hulled tahini

1 cup mashed ripe banana (about 3 small bananas)

1 cup (250 ml) coconut water

TOPPING

1 ripe banana

2 tablespoons cacao

2 tablespoons maple syrup

1 tablespoon hulled tahini

flaked coconut, serve

maple syrup, to serve

Cacao, tahini and maple smoothie

Place all ingredients into a blender and blend on a high speed until smooth and creamy.

Serves 2

1 banana

½ teaspoon cinnamon

1 teaspoon chia seeds

1 tablespoon hemp or flax seeds

2 teaspoons hulled tahini

1 tablespoon cacao powder

1 tablespoon cacao nibs

2 teaspoons maple syrup

2 cups (500 ml) soy, coconut or almond milk

Pitta Recipes

SUMMER
PITTA SEASON

Summer can get pretty hot for Pitta types and keeping cool can be a full-time job if you are not eating the right kinds of food. Pitta heat rises up in the body and can affect all of the doshas. Anyone who has trouble staying cool in summer or throughout the year will benefit from these dishes. Women struggling with hot flushes may also find recipes that provide some relief.

Breakfast

Fruit, coconut and grains are sweet and cooling and are good choices for breakfast for Pittas or anyone looking to stay cool in summer.

Hawaiian coconut French toast

I had the pleasure of finishing this book on the beach in Kauai thanks to my beautiful generous friend Rebecca. I stayed at the St Regis Princeville and spent my days on a beach chair, with chickens wandering past, gazing out at the ocean and writing about the qualities of Vata, Pitta and Kapha. As a Pitta it is important for me to manage heat in my body and my exposure to it (I sat under an umbrella). I have found when I'm on tropical islands and trying to stay cool, I often get great tips from the locals. And, if you haven't already put two and two together, coconut is the perfect Pitta medicine. Its water and flesh are used on nearly every tropical island I have ever visited and if it's summer and I'm not including it in my diet, I notice the heat pretty quickly.

This is a simple brekkie. I've left out the egg yolks here as they can be heating. If you can't find another use for them (I give mine to Cliffy – my dog wonder), then leave them in as the wheat, milk and fruit are cooling.

Whisk together the egg whites and milk in a shallow bowl.

Dip the bread slices in the eggy mixture, making sure they soak it up. Then press each slice in the shredded coconut, covering both sides.

Melt half the ghee in a large non-stick frying pan over medium heat, add two bread slices and cook for 3–5 minutes on each side until golden brown and slightly crispy. Repeat with the remaining ghee and bread.

Serve the French toast drizzled with some coconut yoghurt or maple syrup and topped with your choice of tropical fruit.

Serves 4

3 egg whites, lightly beaten
½ cup (125 ml) unhomogenised milk
4 thick slices of sourdough bread
½ cup (30 g) shredded coconut
3 tablespoons ghee

To serve
coconut yoghurt or pure maple syrup
tropical fruit (such as mango, pineapple, papaya, lime)

Potato rosti with peas and yoghurt

I use coconut yoghurt in this recipe as it is more cooling.

Boil the potatoes until just soft, drain well and allow to cool slightly.

While the potatoes are cooling, melt 1 tablespoon of oil in a frying pan, add the peas and spices and cook, stirring occasionally, over medium heat for 3 minutes, until the spices are fragrant. Remove from the heat, allow to cool, then stir in the mint. Season with salt and pepper.

Grate the potatoes into a bowl. Shape 3 tablespoons of the grated potato into patties, then coat in the cornflour.

Heat a little oil in a large frying pan over medium heat, add the potato rostis in batches and cook for 3 minutes on each side until they are crisp and golden brown. Drain on paper towel.

Whisk the yoghurt with 2 tablespoons of water.

Serve the potato rostis topped with the spiced peas and drizzled with the yoghurt.

Serves 4

500 g floury potatoes (I like to use unwashed potatoes as other types are too waxy), scrubbed

extra-virgin coconut oil, for frying

1 cup (130 g) frozen baby peas

1 teaspoon ground coriander

1 teaspoon ground cumin

½ teaspoon fennel seeds

2 tablespoons chopped mint

sea salt and freshly ground black pepper

3 tablespoons cornflour

⅓ cup (90 g) coconut yoghurt

Watermelon, plum, cherry and pineapple fruit salad

Arrange the fruit in four serving bowls.

Place the mint, coconut sugar, half the pumpkin seeds and the yoghurt in a small blender and blend until smooth.

Serve the fruit topped with the mint yoghurt and finished with the remaining pumpkin seeds.

Serves 4

4 cups (700 g) chopped seedless watermelon

3 plums, sliced

200 g cherries, pitted and halved

2 cups (320 g) chopped pineapple

1 cup (20 g) mint leaves, torn

1 teaspoon coconut sugar

3 tablespoons pumpkin seeds

2 tablespoons coconut yoghurt

Giant coconut pancake with berries and cherries

Preheat the oven to 180°C. Grease and line a 26 cm deep fry pan with baking paper.

Combine the almond meal, coconut flour, desiccated coconut and baking powder in a bowl.

In a separate bowl, whisk together the eggs, rosewater, coconut oil, coconut milk or water and maple syrup.

Make a well in the dry ingredients, pour in the wet ingredients and mix until smooth. Tip into the prepared dish and bake for 30–40 minutes, until set.

Top the pancake with the cherries and berries and drizzle on the extra maple syrup.

Serves 4–6

½ cup (50 g) almond meal

½ cup (60 g) coconut flour

2 tablespoons desiccated coconut

1 teaspoon baking powder

5 eggs

1 tablespoon rosewater

2 tablespoons extra-virgin coconut oil

2½ cups (625 ml) coconut milk or water

2 tablespoons pure maple syrup, plus extra to drizzle

TOPPING

200 g cherries, pitted and halved

200 g mixed fresh berries

Rose semolina cereal with seeds

Uppamma is one of my favourite Indian breakfasts and, sorry, it's not gluten free. Semolina is a wheat product suitable for Pitta types. Rose is cooling, so overheated Pittas might want to make friends with it.

To make the vanilla-infused strawberries, place the strawberries in a bowl, add the vanilla and maple syrup and gently mix to combine. Allow to stand for at least 15 minutes for the flavours to infuse.

Dry roast the semolina in a frying pan for 5 minutes, until light golden; you don't want it to be too brown. Remove from the pan.

Melt the ghee in a large saucepan, add the fennel and cardamom seeds, chana dhal (if using), pumpkin, sunflower and poppy seeds and cook, stirring occasionally, for 3 minutes, until the dhal is golden. Add the lime leaves, rosewater and 3 cups of water and bring to the boil. Cover, reduce the heat to low and simmer for 10 minutes.

Add the roasted semolina to the pan, stirring until the mixture is smooth. Bring to the boil, reduce the heat and simmer, covered, for 3 minutes. Remove from the heat, stir, then cover and allow to stand for 5 minutes before serving.

Serve mounds of the cereal with a drizzle of maple syrup and a side of vanilla-infused strawberries.

Serves 4

1 cup (180 g) fine semolina

2 tablespoons ghee

1 teaspoon fennel seeds

1 teaspoon green cardamom seeds

1 tablespoon chana dhal (optional)

2 tablespoons pumpkin seeds

2 tablespoons sunflower seeds

1 tablespoon poppy seeds

4 kaffir lime leaves, lightly crushed

1 tablespoon rosewater

VANILLA-INFUSED STRAWBERRIES

250 g fresh strawberries, halved

½ teaspoon vanilla powder or natural vanilla extract

2 teaspoons pure maple syrup, plus extra to drizzle

Smoothie bowls

Place the avocado, banana, coconut cream and maple syrup in a high-speed blender and blend until smooth.

Transfer the mixture to serving bowls and serve immediately, topped with the fruit, goji berries, seeds and coconut.

Serves 4

2 partially frozen peeled avocados

2 frozen ripe bananas

1 cup (250 ml) coconut cream, chilled

2 tablespoons pure maple syrup

2 tamarillo. sliced

1 mango, sliced

2 kiwi fruit, sliced

3 tablespoons goji berries

2 tablespoons pumpkin seeds

2 tablespoons chia seeds

2 tablespoons shredded coconut

Mixed grain porridge with coconut whip

To make the coconut whip, place one can of coconut cream in the refrigerator to chill overnight, do not shake the can: you want the coconut cream to settle at the top of the tin. The next morning, open the can, scoop the coconut cream from the top and put it into a bowl; reserve the coconut liquid to use in the porridge. Add the vanilla and maple syrup to the coconut cream and beat with electric beaters until soft peaks form; cover and refrigerate while you cook the porridge.

Dry roast the grains in a large frying pan over medium heat for 5 minutes, until browned and smelling toasted.

Tip the grains into a saucepan, add the ginger, apple, dates and 3 cups of water and bring to the boil. Cook over medium–high heat for 40–50 minutes, until the grains are soft and nearly all the liquid has been absorbed.

Add the cinnamon, cardamom, fennel and reserved coconut liquid to the porridge and cook over medium heat for 5 minutes, until warmed through.

Serve bowls of the porridge topped with the coconut whip, ghee, berries, figs, seeds and a drizzle of maple syrup.

Serves 4

TIPS: *You could cook the grains in a rice cooker, as they all take the same amount of time to cook. If you don't have red rice, use wild rice.*

COCONUT WHIP

2 x 400 ml cans coconut cream

½ teaspoon vanilla powder or 1 teaspoon natural vanilla extract

1 tablespoon pure maple syrup, plus extra to drizzle

PORRIDGE

½ cup (50 g) red rice

½ cup (100 g) barley

¼ cup (95 g) brown rice

1 tablespoon grated fresh ginger

3 apples, grated

6 medjool dates, pitted and roughly chopped

2 teaspoons ground cinnamon

2 teaspoons ground cardamom

1 teaspoon ground fennel

To serve

2 tablespoons ghee

200 g mixed fresh berries

4 figs, torn in half

2 tablespoons flaxseeds

2 tablespoons pumpkin seeds

Peas 3 ways

ZUCCHINI AND PEA FRITTERS

Place the peas, zucchini and mint in a bowl.

Whisk together the egg whites and flour until smooth. Pour into the pea mixture and mix to combine. Fold in the cheese.

Heat the oil in a frying pan over medium heat and, in batches of 3–4, drop in tablespoons of the batter and cook until bubbles appear and burst on the surface. Turn and cook on the other side until golden brown and cooked through. Serve with the lemon wedges.

Serves 4

1 cup (130 g) frozen baby peas, thawed, lightly mashed

1 cup (135 g) grated zucchini

1 tablespoon finely chopped mint

3 egg whites

¼ cup (45 g) rice flour or gluten-free flour

50 g cottage cheese or goat's cheese

extra-virgin coconut oil, for frying

lemon wedges, to serve

COCONUT MINTY PEAS

Heat the oil in a saucepan over medium heat. Add the cumin and cook for 1 minute or until the spice is fragrant. Add the peas and coconut cream and cook over medium heat to warm the peas. Remove from the heat, add the mint and salt, and mash lightly to crush the peas.

Serves 2–4

1 tablespoon coconut oil

1 teaspoon ground cumin

2 cups (260 g) frozen baby peas, thawed

1 cup (250 ml) coconut cream

2 tablespoons chopped mint

pinch of sea salt

WARM PEAS, BRUSSELS SPROUTS AND LETTUCE

Steam the brussels sprouts in a colander over a saucepan of simmering water until bright green and tender, about 5–7 minutes.

Melt the ghee in a frying pan over medium heat, add the brussels sprouts, peas and lettuce and cook to heat the peas through and soften the lettuce. Add the mirin and tamari and cook for 2 minutes.

Serves 4

200 g baby brussels sprouts, halved

3 tablespoons ghee

1 cup (130 g) frozen baby peas, thawed

2 cups (100 g) shredded cos lettuce

1 tablespoon mirin

1 tablespoon tamari

Lunch

Pumpkin patties with coconut cabbage salad

The chia soaks up the moisture in the patty, so when you shape them, things might get a bit messy. Sorry about that. They do really need to stand for 30 minutes at least to give the chia time to bind them.

Place the pumpkin, chickpeas, lime leaves, lemongrass, chilli sauce, lime zest, chia seeds, coconut, coconut flour and egg in a bowl and mix well. Shape ¼-cup portions of the mixture into eight patties. Allow to stand for 30 minutes (this allows time for the chia seeds to soak up any excess moisture in the patties).

Place the poppy seeds in a shallow dish. Press the patties in the poppy seeds, shaking off any excess.

Heat the oil in a large non-stick frying pan over medium heat. Cook the patties in batches until browned on both sides and warmed through, 3–5 minutes on each side. Drain on paper towel. Keep warm.

To make the salad, place the salad ingredients in a bowl and gently toss.

Whisk the dressing ingredients together in a small bowl, pour over the salad and toss to coat. Serve the patties topped with the salad and lime wedges.

Serves 4

1 cup (250 g) grated pumpkin

1 x 400 g can chickpeas, rinsed, drained and mashed

6 kaffir lime leaves, finely shredded

2 lemongrass stems, pale part only, pounded to a paste

1 tablespoon sweet chilli sauce

zest of 1 lime

2 tablespoons chia seeds

½ cup (45 g) desiccated coconut

½ cup (70 g) coconut flour

1 egg, lightly beaten

¼ cup (40 g) poppy seeds

extra-virgin coconut oil, for frying

lime wedges, to serve

COCONUT CABBAGE SALAD

½ Chinese cabbage (wombok), very thinly sliced

3 spring onions, sliced

100 g bean sprouts

100 g mung bean sprouts

1 cup (20 g) coriander leaves

DRESSING

2 tablespoons extra-virgin coconut oil

2 tablespoons lime juice

1 tablespoon tamari

2 teaspoons coconut sugar

San choy bau

The quickled (that's a fancy word for fast pickled) vegetables dress up this dish and give it a bit of colour.

Place the carrot, capsicum and bean sprouts in a bowl with the vinegar, sugar and ½ cup of water. Allow to pickle while you prepare your mince.

Melt the oil in a frying pan, add the mince and cook over medium heat until browned, breaking up any lumps with a wooden spoon as it cooks. Add the bamboo shoots, water chestnuts and oyster sauce and cook until warmed through.

Spoon the mince mixture into the lettuce leaves, top with some carrot, capsicum and sprout pickle and roll up to enclose.

Serves 4

TIP: *You can use cabbage instead of iceberg lettuce leaves.*

1 carrot, thinly sliced

1 red capsicum, thinly sliced

50 g bean sprouts

2 tablespoons rice vinegar

1 teaspoon coconut sugar

1 tablespoon extra-virgin coconut oil

500 g turkey or chicken mince

1 x 230 g can bamboo shoots, drained

1 x 230 g can water chestnuts, drained and roughly chopped

2 tablespoons oyster sauce

iceberg lettuce leaves, washed

Chargrilled fennel and fish with herbed avocado

In Ayurveda we roast or soak grains to make them more digestible and I think not doing this as a standard practice is where we have come a little unstuck with grains and why we have so much trouble digesting them.

Heat the barbecue to hot.

Dry roast the pearl barley in a small frying pan for 5 minutes, until golden brown and smelling nutty.

Bring a saucepan of water to the boil, add the pearl barley and cook for 30–40 minutes, until soft. Rinse under cold water and drain well. Place in a bowl and add the leafy greens.

While the barley is cooking, toss the asparagus, fennel and leek in the oil and cook on the barbecue for 5–10 minutes, until soft. The asparagus spears will take the least time to cook, so add them last.

Whisk together the dressing ingredients in a small bowl, pour over the vegetables and toss to combine.

Squeeze the lime juice over the avocado, then lightly press the avocado wedges in the dill to coat.

Pile the barley and leafy greens onto a serving plate, top with the chargrilled vegetables, smoked fish and herbed avocado.

Serves 4

½ cup (100 g) pearl barley

100 g leafy greens (such as curly kale, rocket, chicory, mizuna, beetroot leaves), rinsed

1 bunch of asparagus (about 250 g), woody ends trimmed

1 fennel bulb, thinly sliced

2 leeks, pale part only, thickly sliced

2 tablespoons olive oil

2 tablespoons lime juice

2 avocados, cut into thick wedges

a handful of chopped dill

200 g boneless smoked fish, broken into bite-size pieces

DRESSING

3 tablespoons extra-virgin olive oil

1½ teaspoons roasted fennel seeds, crushed

1½ tablespoons apple cider vinegar

1½ teaspoons pure maple syrup

Bun bowls

To make the lemongrass chicken, pound the lemongrass and coriander root to a paste using a mortar and pestle. Transfer to a shallow dish, add the coconut water, fish sauce, sugar and oil and mix well. Add the chicken and turn to coat in the marinade. Cover and refrigerate overnight or as long as time permits.

Whisk the dressing ingredients with ⅓ cup of water in a jug. Add the cucumber and carrot and allow to pickle while you cook the chicken.

Return the chicken to room temperature 30 minutes before cooking. Drain the chicken and pat dry with paper towel.

Heat a barbecue grill to medium–hot. Chargrill the chicken for 10 minutes, until tender and cooked through. (Alternatively, cook under a grill or in a chargrill pan.)

Meanwhile, pour boiling water over the vermicelli and allow to stand for 10 minutes, until soft. Drain well.

Pile the vermicelli onto a platter, top with the chicken, carrot, cucumber, sprouts, coriander and fried shallots. Drizzle the dressing over the top and serve.

Serves 4

100 g fine rice vermicelli

2 carrots, finely shredded

2 Lebanese cucumbers, finely shredded

1 cup (160 g) bean sprouts

1 cup (20 g) coriander sprigs

2 tablespoons fried shallots

LEMONGRASS CHICKEN

2 lemongrass stems, pale part only, finely chopped

1 tablespoon chopped coriander root

2 tablespoons coconut water

2 tablespoons fish sauce

1 teaspoon coconut sugar

1 tablespoon extra-virgin coconut oil, melted

2 chicken breast fillets, sliced

DRESSING

2 tablespoons fish sauce

2 tablespoons sweet chilli sauce

2 tablespoons lime juice

Sushi bowl

Place the brown and wild rice in a saucepan, add 3 cups of water and bring to the boil over high heat. Continue to boil for 20 minutes, until tunnels form in the rice and most of the liquid has been absorbed. Reduce the heat to low, cover and cook for 5 minutes more until the rice is soft and there is no liquid left in the pan. Remove from the heat, stir in the tamari and mirin with a large spoon and allow to sit while you prepare the toppings.

Whisk the egg whites, poppy seeds, pumpkin seeds and sesame oil together in a bowl. Heat the coconut oil in a non-stick frying pan over medium heat, add the egg white mixture and cook until the edge begins to set. Then, using a spatula, gently push the cooked egg on the outside of the pan to the centre and tilt the pan to allow any unset egg to run to the edge of the pan. Continue doing this until all the egg is set. Remove the seed omelette from the pan and shred.

Divide the rice between four serving bowls, then decoratively arrange the avocado, cucumber, broccoli, edamame, seed omelette, nori and pickled ginger on top.

Serves 4

1 cup (200 g) brown basmati rice

½ cup (95 g) wild rice

1 tablespoon tamari

1 tablespoon mirin

3 egg whites

1 tablespoon poppy seeds

1 tablespoon pumpkin seeds

½ teaspoon toasted sesame oil

1 tablespoon extra-virgin coconut oil, melted

2 avocados, thinly sliced

1 Lebanese cucumber, thinly sliced

200 g broccoli, cut into florets, steamed

1 cup (120 g) frozen shelled edamame, thawed

2 nori sheets

3 tablespoons sweet pickled ginger

Green mung dosa with coconut chutney

These dosas make a fabulous alternative to wraps. You will need a good blender to puree the soaked beans.

Soak the mung dhal in cold water overnight. Rinse and drain well.

Place the mung dhal in a high-speed blender with the coriander and ginger and blend. Add enough water to form a thin paste.

Transfer the mixture to a bowl, add the flour and a pinch of salt and mix to make a thin pouring batter.

Heat a little ghee in a 20 cm non-stick frying pan over medium heat, add 3 tablespoons of batter and very quickly, using the back of a big spoon, swirl around to form a large pancake. Cook for 3–5 minutes, until bubbles appear and burst on the surface and the pancake is easy to flip over. Turn and cook the other side until the pancake is dry and golden. Repeat with the remaining ghee and batter.

Place the coconut chutney ingredients in the blender, add 1 tablespoon of water and a pinch of salt and blend until smooth.

Serve the dosas with the coconut chutney, fennel seeds and mango chutney.

1 cup (225 g) split green mung dhal

a handful of coriander leaves

1 tablespoon grated ginger

2 teaspoons rice flour

sea salt

3 tablespoons ghee

1 teaspoon fennel seeds

mango chutney, to serve

QUICK COCONUT CHUTNEY

½ cup (45 g) desiccated coconut

1 tablespoon coconut yoghurt

½ small green chilli, halved lengthways and seeded

1 teaspoon grated ginger

Makes 8

Chickpea crêpes with ricotta, egg, cress and caramelised onion

Sift the flour and bicarbonate of soda into a bowl, add the seeds, spice, salt and mint and mix to combine. Make a well in the centre, pour in the coconut water and mix until you have a thin smooth batter.

Melt 1 teaspoon of coconut oil in a non-stick frying pan over medium heat, add 3 tablespoons of batter per crêpe and cook until bubbles appear on the surface, about 3 minutes. Turn and cook on the other side for 2 minutes. Transfer to a warm plate and keep warm while you cook the remaining crêpes. You should end up with 12 in total.

Melt 1 tablespoon of coconut oil in the frying pan you used to cook the crêpes, add the onion and cook, stirring occasionally, over medium heat for 10 minutes, until the onion is soft. Stir in the sugar and cook for 5 minutes, until the onion is sticky and caramelised.

Serve the crêpes topped with the ricotta, egg, cress and caramelised onion.

1½ cups (165 g) chickpea flour (besan)

2 teaspoons bicarbonate of soda

1½ teaspoons cumin seeds

1 teaspoon fennel seeds

1 teaspoon ground turmeric

pinch of sea salt

2 tablespoons finely chopped mint

1½ cups (375 ml) coconut water

extra-virgin coconut oil, for frying

2 red onions, thinly sliced

1 teaspoon coconut sugar

250 g fresh ricotta

4 hard-boiled eggs, peeled and sliced

a handful of cress sprouts

Serves 4

TIP: *You could also use herbed paneer (page 141) instead of the ricotta.*

Roasted cauliflower, potato and kale salad

I feel pretty sure you will make this simple salad – created from two of my all-time favourite vegetable snacks – time and time again. Potato and cauliflower are both cooling vegetables, perfect for Pitta types.

Preheat the oven to 200°C. Line two baking trays with baking paper.

Place the cauliflower and potatoes on one baking tray, sprinkle on the turmeric, fennel seeds and salt, drizzle on 2 tablespoons of melted coconut oil and toss to coat. Bake for 45 minutes, until the cauliflower is starting to blacken in parts (make sure you cook it well or it will be watery) and the potatoes are tender.

Reduce the oven temperature to 180°C.

Combine the remaining melted coconut oil and tamari in a large bowl, add the kale and toss. Place on the other baking tray and bake for 10 minutes, until the kale is crisp. Remove from the tray.

Combine the kale, cauliflower and potatoes in a large serving bowl and gently toss.

Serves 4

1 head of cauliflower, cut into florets

300 g baby potatoes, halved if they are not really small

1 teaspoon ground turmeric

1 teaspoon fennel seeds

sea salt

⅓ cup (80 ml) melted extra-virgin coconut oil

2 teaspoons tamari

1 bunch of kale (about 300 g), central stems removed, leaves torn into large pieces

Green pasta with peas and soft mozzarella

Avoid using too much parmesan as it is a hard cheese and hard cheeses tend to heat Pittas up. You decide if you want to use gluten-free pasta, but wheat is cooling and suitable for Pittas.

Half fill a large saucepan with water and bring to the boil, add the tagliatelle and kale. Once the kale has turned bright green, 2–3 minutes, remove with tongs and set aside. Once the pasta is cooked, drain well, reserving 1 cup of the cooking liquid.

Place the garlic, basil, lemon zest and juice, half the parmesan and the peas in a food processor and process until smooth. Season with salt and pepper.

Place the drained pasta in serving bowls, add the kale and the pea puree and toss well to coat the pasta. Serve the pasta topped with the burrata or bocconcini and the remaining parmesan.

Serves 4

300 g tagliatelle

1 bunch of kale (about 300 g), central stems removed

2 garlic cloves, peeled

1 cup (20 g) basil leaves

zest and juice of 1 lemon

½ cup (50 g) grated parmesan

1 cup (140 g) frozen peas

sea salt and freshly ground black pepper

200 g burrata or bocconcini, torn

Leafy greens 3 ways

KALE PARATHA

Steam the kale in a steamer or colander set over a saucepan of simmering water until bright green and tender, 3–5 minutes. Allow to cool.

Place the flour in a bowl and add chilli, ajwain, salt and 2 teaspoons of ghee and mix to combine.

Stir in the kale and 3 cups of water and mix to form a smooth dough.

Shape tablespoons of the mixture into balls. Roll each ball out on a lightly floured surface, brush the surface with ghee then fold in all sides to form a square.

Heat the ghee on a flat plate or in a large frypan, cook the parathas over a medium high heat until golden brown on both sides.

Serve with yoghurt and lime pickle.

1 small bunch of kale (about 200 g), central stems removed, leaves finely chopped

2 cups atta or wheat flour

1 green chilli, seeds removed (optional)

1 teaspoon ajwain seeds

salt

2 teaspoons ghee, plus extra for frying

yoghurt and lime pickle to serve

LETTUCE WEDGES AND CUCUMBER WITH MINT DRESSING

Cut the lettuce into wedges, halve the cucumbers and arrange on a platter. Crush the mint in a mortar and pestle.

Combine the mint with the lime juice and avocado oil and drizzle over the lettuce and cucumber.

1 iceberg lettuce

4 small cucumbers

handful of mint

1 tablespoon lime juice

1 tablespoon avocado oil

LETTUCE LEAVES WITH AVOCADO AND CUCUMBER DIP

Place the avocado, cucumber, cumin, turmeric, salt, garlic and yoghurt in a bowl and mix to combine. Serve on baby cos lettuce boats topped with alfalfa.

Serves 4

1 avocado, mashed

1 Lebanese cucumber, roughly chopped

1 teaspoon ground cumin

½ teaspoon ground turmeric

pinch of sea salt

1 garlic clove, grated

1 cup (250 g) unsweetened coconut yoghurt

2 baby cos lettuce, separated into leaves

alfalfa sprouts, to serve

Dinner

Avocado, egg and nori rice paper rolls

Put the vermicelli in a heatproof bowl, cover with boiling water and allow to stand for 10 minutes, until the noodles are soft. Drain well and cut into shorter lengths.

Working with one wrapper at a time, immerse the rice paper in a shallow bowl of lukewarm water until the rice paper is just soft. Lay the rice paper on a clean tea towel on a chopping board, top with 2 mint leaves, a strip of nori, 1 heaped tablespoon of vermicelli, a few slices of egg, some cucumber, avocado and carrot.

Wrap the rice paper around the filling, folding in the sides and rolling until completely enclosed. Cover and keep moist under a slightly damp piece of paper towel while you prepare the remaining rolls.

Whisk the dipping sauce ingredients in a small bowl.

Place the rice paper rolls on a platter and serve with the dipping sauce or hoisin sauce.

Makes 12

50 g thin rice vermicelli

12 rice paper wrappers (about 22 cm diameter)

24 mint leaves

2 nori sheets, cut into 12 strips

3 hard-boiled eggs, sliced

1 Lebanese cucumber, cut into thin strips

2 avocados, sliced

2 carrots, cut into thin sticks

DIPPING SAUCE

½ teaspoon toasted sesame oil

2 tablespoons rice vinegar

2 tablespoons lime juice

1–2 teaspoons coconut sugar

2 tablespoons water

Cooling cucumber and strawberry mint coconut water

Sparkling mineral water is very cooling so limit its consumption to hot summer days.

Place the cucumber, mint, strawberries and coconut water in a tall jug and mix to combine.

Serves 4

½ Lebanese cucumber, thinly sliced

handful of mint leaves, bruised

100 g strawberries, sliced

4 cups (1 litre) coconut or sparkling water

Herbed paneer with pressed cabbage, radish and cucumber salad

This recipe takes a few hours, but is well worth the wait. Pressed salads are simple, they just need a bit of time for the salt to extract the liquid from the vegetables.

Place the milk in a saucepan, bring to the boil, add the lemon juice and stir until the mixture separates into curds and whey, about 5–10 minutes. If the mixture doesn't split, you may need to add a bit more lemon juice. Strain through a sieve lined with muslin set over a bowl and squeeze out any excess moisture. Stir the herbs, fennel and a pinch of salt into the curds in the sieve, then tie off the muslin with a rubber band and leave to drain in the fridge for 1-2 hours, or more if you want a very firm paneer. (Pour the whey into an airtight container and keep in the fridge for smoothies.)

Place the cabbage, radish, cucumber and carrot in a bowl. Add the vinegar and salt and mix to combine. Cover with a plate and weigh down with a bowl filled with water or a few cans. Set aside for 1 hour.

Place the basil oil ingredients in a food processor, add 2 tablespoons of water and process until smooth.

Serve the sliced paneer with the pressed salad and a drizzle of the basil oil.

Serves 4

2 litres unhomogenised cow's milk
juice of 1 lemon, plus extra if needed
3 tablespoons chopped dill
3 tablespoons chopped mint
1 teaspoon roasted fennel seeds
pinch of sea salt

SALAD

1 cup (75 g) finely shredded savoy cabbage
6 radishes, thinly sliced
6 baby cucumbers, thinly sliced
2 carrots, thinly sliced
2 tablespoons rice vinegar
2 teaspoons sea salt

BASIL OIL

1 cup (20 g) basil and parsley leaves
1 garlic clove, chopped
2 tablespoons extra-virgin olive oil

Mushroom and basil tart

Another recipe requiring patience, which Pitta types can often lack. Serve with a leafy green salad.

Preheat the oven to 200°C. Grease and line a 20 cm tart tin with a removable base with baking paper.

To make the tart shell, place the almond meal, chickpea flour, basil and a pinch of salt in a bowl and mix to combine. In a separate bowl, whisk together the oil and eggs and pour over the dry ingredients. Stir to bring the dough together, then press together with your hands.

Roll out the dough between two sheets of baking paper until it is large enough to cover the base and side of the prepared tin. Place the pastry in the tin and rest for 30 minutes in the freezer. Cover with baking paper and top with rice or baking beans. Bake for 30 minutes, until the base is crisp and golden. Remove the paper and baking weights. Set aside to cool completely.

To make the filling, place the cashews in a food processor, add the nutritional yeast, garlic, lemon juice, ghee or oil, rocket, basil and ½ cup of water and process until smooth and creamy.

Pour the filling into the tart shell and chill for 2 hours until set. Return the tart to room temperature 20 minutes before serving.

Heat the oil and ghee in a frying pan over high heat, add the garlic and mushrooms and cook, stirring occasionally, until the mushrooms are browned, about 5 minutes. Stir in the tamari and remove from the heat. Spoon on top of the cashew filling.

Serves 6–8

2 tablespoons olive oil

1 tablespoon ghee

2 garlic cloves, crushed

500 g mixed button, oyster and Swiss brown mushrooms, sliced

1 tablespoon tamari

TART SHELL

1 cup (100 g) almond meal

1 cup (110 g) chickpea flour (besan)

1 tablespoon chopped basil

sea salt

2 tablespoons extra-virgin olive oil or melted coconut oil

2 eggs

FILLING

1 cup (150 g) cashew nuts, soaked in cold water for 2 hours, drained

2 tablespoons nutritional yeast

1 garlic clove, peeled

juice of 1 lemon

2 tablespoons ghee or extra-virgin coconut oil

1 cup (50 g) wild rocket leaves

2 tablespoons chopped basil

Sweet potato gnocchi with lemony fennel, broccoli and ghee sauce

Roast your sweet potatoes whole in their skins for this recipe, no oil needed. When cool, peel away the skins and you will be left with deliciously sweeter-than-sweet sweet potato.

Put the sweet potato, flour, LSA, salt and egg white into a bowl and mix to form a soft dough. If it is a little sticky, add a touch more flour but be careful not to make it too dry.

Roll tablespoons of the dough into balls, flatten slightly and place on a tray lined with baking paper.

To make the sauce, combine the ghee, fennel seeds, herbs, broccoli and lemon zest in a large frying pan and cook over medium–high heat until the ghee turns a nutty brown colour and the broccoli is soft. Reduce the heat to low, add the lemon juice and simmer for 5 minutes.

Bring a large saucepan of water to the boil, add the gnocchi in batches and cook until they rise to the surface. Remove with a slotted spoon and transfer to warm serving bowls.

Serve the gnocchi topped with the goat's cheese.

Serves 2–4

750 g mashed roast sweet potato

1 cup (120 g) coconut or gluten-free flour

¼ cup (25 g) LSA (you can use any nut meal)

a good pinch of sea salt

1 egg white

LEMONY FENNEL, BROCCOLI AND GHEE SAUCE

½ cup (125 g) ghee

1 teaspoon fennel seeds

2 tablespoons mixed oregano and thyme leaves, chopped

1 head of broccoli, grated

zest and juice of 1 juicy lemon

To serve

goat's cheese

Green falafel with mint yoghurt tahini

I've made a lot of falafel mixes in my time but, I have to say, this is one of the tastiest and easiest – the falafels are baked rather than deep-fried. The mix is soft and stays together and has a beautiful texture that isn't dry. I'm not a massive fan of canned beans but canned chickpeas make this recipe much quicker than using the dried alternative.

Preheat the oven to 200°C. Line a baking tray with baking paper.

Place the herbs, pumpkin seeds, chickpeas, garlic, onion, cumin and baking powder in a food processor and process until smooth. Add the olive oil, season and pulse until the mixture is combined. Transfer to a bowl and shape tablespoons of the mixture into 16 balls, flatten slightly. Place the falafels on the lined tray, lightly brush with the extra oil and bake for 15–20 minutes, until golden.

Combine the mint yoghurt tahini ingredients in a food processor, add 2 tablespoons of water and process until smooth.

Serve the falafel balls in the cabbage or lettuce leaves topped with the cucumber and drizzled with the mint yoghurt tahini.

Serves 4

1 cup (20 g) flat-leaf parsley leaves

1 cup (20 g) mint leaves

½ cup (125 g) pumpkin seeds

2 x 400 g cans chickpeas, rinsed and drained well

2 garlic cloves, chopped

1 small red onion, chopped

1 teaspoon ground cumin

1 teaspoon baking powder

sea salt and freshly ground black pepper

2 tablespoons olive oil, plus extra for brushing

soft cabbage or lettuce leaves, to serve

2 Lebanese cucumbers, chopped

MINT YOGHURT TAHINI

1 cup (250 g) coconut yoghurt

1 tablespoon hulled tahini

1 cup (20 g) mint leaves

1 garlic clove, chopped

Marinated chicken with coconut lime dressing

Place the chicken, turmeric, garlic, yoghurt, spices, onion and lime juice in a shallow bowl and mix well to coat the chicken. Cover and refrigerate for as long as time permits; overnight is ideal.

The next day, combine the coconut lime dressing ingredients in a bowl, add the water and mix well.

Bring the chicken drumsticks to room temperature 30 minutes before cooking.

Preheat oven to 200°C. Line a baking tray with baking paper and place chicken on the tray. Cook the drumsticks, turning several times, for 40–50 minutes, until cooked through.

Serve the chicken topped with the coconut lime dressing.

Serves 4–6

1.5 kg chicken drumsticks, scored

1 teaspoon ground turmeric

2 garlic cloves, chopped

½ cup (125 g) coconut yoghurt

1 teaspoon each of ground coriander, ground cumin, sweet paprika and garam masala

1 small red onion, grated

1 tablespoon lime juice

COCONUT LIME DRESSING

2 tablespoons desiccated coconut

zest and juice of 2 limes

1 teaspoon coconut sugar

1 small green chilli, seeded and chopped

2 tablespoons finely chopped coriander

3 tablespoons avocado or coconut oil

2 tablespoons water

Filled capsicums

Place the rice, oil, onion, coriander, parsley, lemon zest, baharat and 2 cups of water in a saucepan and bring to the boil. Reduce the heat and simmer for 15 minutes, until the rice is soft and all the liquid has been absorbed.

Transfer the rice to a bowl and set aside to cool while you prepare the capsicum.

Preheat the oven to 180°C. Choose a roasting tin that fits the capsicums snugly.

Cut the tops off the capsicums and reserve, then pull out and discard the membrane and seeds. Fill each capsicum with the cooled rice mixture, place the capsicum lids on top and place upright in the roasting tin. Pour ½ cup of water into the tin and bake for 40 minutes, until the capsicum skins are soft and shrunken.

Serves 4

NOTE: *Baharat, also known as Lebanese 7 spice, is a traditional complex sweet and smoky Middle Eastern spice mix. You can buy it from delis, some supermarkets and online.*

1 cup (200 g) white rice

1 tablespoon olive oil

1 small red onion, chopped

2 tablespoons chopped coriander

2 tablespoons chopped flat-leaf parsley

zest of 1 lemon

2 teaspoons baharat (see Note)

4 small red capsicums

Cooling dhal with tempered spices

This is more of a wintery dhal for Pitta types, as it does have a few warming spices. If you are making it in summer, leave out the mustard seeds and chilli.

Soak the dhal in cold water overnight (this helps to make them more digestible). Rinse and drain.

Place the dhal, bay leaves, turmeric, ground coriander, garam masala, salt and 1.5 litres of water in a large saucepan and bring to the boil. Reduce the heat to low and simmer, covered, for 50 minutes, until the dhal are soft and mushy. Check and stir regularly to ensure the dhal are not catching on the bottom of the pan. I use a potato masher to mash them but don't overdo it, you don't want a puree.

Once the dhal are cooked, heat the ghee in a frying pan, add the spices and cook over medium heat for 3 minutes, until they are fragrant and the mustard seeds start to pop. Remove from the heat.

Divide the dhal between serving bowls, and swirl a little of the tempered spices into each bowl before serving. Finish with a good squeeze of lime juice and a sprinkle of coriander leaves and coconut.

Serves 4

1½ cups (375 g) chana dhal

2 bay leaves

1½ teaspoons ground turmeric

2 teaspoons ground coriander

2 teaspoons garam masala

sea salt

3 tablespoons ghee

2 teaspoons cumin seeds

1 teaspoon fennel seeds

1 teaspoon black mustard seeds

3 cloves

1 cinnamon stick, broken

1 dried chilli

¼ cup (25 g) shredded coconut

2 limes, halved

coriander leaves, to serve

Winter fish curry

A lovely winter fish curry for Pitta types.

Cut the fish into large bite-sized pieces and pat dry.

Melt the oil in a large, deep frying pan, add the onion and cook over medium heat for 10 minutes, until golden. Add the garlic and spices and cook until the spices are fragrant. Tip in the coconut cream and tomato and bring to the boil. Reduce the heat and simmer for 15 minutes, until the oil starts to separate. Add the fish and broccoli, cover and cook for 5 minutes. Add the snow peas, cover and cook for 2 minutes, until the snow peas are bright green and tender-crisp and the fish is just cooked through.

Serve the fish curry with the Ghee infused with Vata-calming spices with basmati rice (page 100).

Serves 4

500 g fish fillets (such as kingfish or barramundi), pin-boned

2 tablespoons extra-virgin coconut oil

1 red onion, chopped

2 garlic cloves, chopped

1 tablespoon grated ginger

1 teaspoon each of black mustard seeds, fennel seeds, ground turmeric and garam masala

1 cinnamon stick

1 large green chilli, halved lengthways

8 curry leaves

1 x 400 ml can coconut cream

2 tomatoes, chopped

200 g broccoli, cut into florets

100 g snow peas, trimmed

Coconut 3 ways

COCONUT ROSE LASSI

Place the coconut cream, yoghurt and ¾ cup of water in a blender and blend until smooth. Add the rosewater, coriander and dates or maple syrup and blend until smooth and creamy.

Serves 2

½ cup (125 ml) coconut cream

½ cup (125 g) coconut yoghurt or plain yoghurt

1 tablespoon rosewater

2 teaspoons ground coriander

3 pitted medjool dates or 1 tablespoon pure maple syrup

COCONUT CHICKEN PIECES

Preheat the oven to 180°C. Line a baking tray with baking paper.

Whisk together the egg whites, coconut cream, lime zest and juice.

Dip the chicken in the cornflour, then in the egg mixture, then toss to coat in the shredded coconut. Drizzle on the coconut oil and place the chicken on the lined tray. Bake for 20 minutes, until the chicken is cooked through and the coconut is golden brown. Serve with the salad.

Serves 4

2 egg whites

2 tablespoons coconut cream

1 teaspoon lime zest

1 tablespoon lime juice

500 g chicken tenderloins

½ cup (60 g) cornflour or potato starch

1½ cups (90 g) shredded coconut

3 tablespoons melted extra-virgin coconut oil

finely shredded cabbage and lime and coriander salad, to serve

CHICKPEA AND POPPY SEED COCONUT CURRY

If using the dried chickpeas, soak in cold water overnight, then rinse and drain. Cook in boiling water for 40 minutes, until just tender. Drain well.

Heat the oil in a frying pan, add the poppy seeds and cook over medium heat until they start to pop. Stir in the spices and coconut and cook until the spices are fragrant.

Transfer the seeds and spice mixture to a small food processor and process with 2–3 tablespoons of water until you have a smooth paste.

Return the paste to the pan, stir in the tomato, potato, peas, chickpeas and coconut cream, cover and cook over low heat for 20 minutes, until the curry is thick and creamy and the potato is soft. Season with a little salt and serve with rice.

Serves 4

1½ cups dried chickpeas, or 2 x 400 g cans chickpeas, drained and rinsed

2 tablespoons extra-virgin coconut oil

1 teaspoon poppy seeds

1 teaspoon each of garam masala, ground coriander, ground turmeric

1 cinnamon stick

¾ cup (65 g) desiccated coconut

1 tomato, chopped

2 potatoes, peeled and chopped

1 cup (130 g) frozen baby peas

1 x 400 ml can coconut cream

sea salt

steamed basmati rice, to serve

Sweet treats, snacks and drinks

Watermelon, elderflower, rose and kaffir lime spritzer

Place the watermelon, rosewater, cordial, lime zest and juice and kaffir lime leaves in a tall jug and mix with a wooden spoon to combine the flavours. Add the mineral water and serve.

Serves 4

1 cup (200 g) roughly chopped seedless watermelon

2 teaspoons rosewater

3 tablespoons elderflower and pomegranate cordial

zest and juice of 1 lime

6 kaffir lime leaves, bruised

4 cups (1 litre) sparkling mineral water

Cooling pineapple, passionfruit and jasmine tea

Place the passionfruit juice, pineapple juice, lime juice and jasmine tea in a tall jug and mix to combine.

Serves 4

1 cup (250 ml) passionfruit juice

2 cups (500 ml) pineapple juice

1 tablespoon lime juice

2 cups (500 ml) cooled jasmine tea

Poached plums with elderflower and spices

Place the spices, elderflower cordial and 2 cups (500 ml) water into a pan and bring to boil. Add the plums, cover and cook for 10–15 minutes or until the fruit is just soft but not mushy.

Add the sugar and cook for 5 minutes more.

Remove the plums from the poaching liquid and spoon the plums into a sterilised wide-mouthed bottle, and scatter the elderflowers over the top.

Bring the poaching liquid to boil and cook over a high heat for 15 minutes or until the liquid has reduced and thickened slightly. Pour over the plums and seal.

Makes 2 litres

1 vanilla bean or 1 teaspoon vanilla powder

2 star anise

4 cloves

1 bay leaf

1 cinnamon stick

½ cup (60 ml) elderflower cordial

2 kg red plums (not too ripe or they will break apart when you cook them)

1½ cups (375 g) coconut sugar

handful of fresh elderflowers

Proper apple pie

A classic cooling dessert for Pitta types. The shortcrust pastry uses cooling wheat and apples are a cooling fruit best eaten cooked as they can be tricky to digest.

To make the pastry, rub the butter or ghee into the flour until the mixture resembles fine breadcrumbs. Add the sugar and mix to combine. Gradually add ½ cup of water and stir with a flat-bladed knife until the mixture comes together. Shape the dough into a ball. Most people at this point chill the pastry, I don't as I find chilled pastry a pain in the neck to roll out.

Divide the pastry into two portions. Roll out one portion between two sheets of baking paper until it is large enough to cover the base and side of a 22 cm pie tin. Place the pastry in the tin and chill in the freezer while you prepare the pie filling. If it's a hot day, chill the other portion of dough.

To make the filling, peel and core the apples. Cut half of them into large pieces and the rest into small chunks. Melt the ghee in a large saucepan, add the apple, lemon juice, rosemary, vanilla, saffron, cinnamon and sugar and cook for 10 minutes, until the apple softens. Remove from the pan and allow to cool. (Using hot apples in the filling will leave you with a soggy pastry bottom, so please don't be tempted to rush this part.) Remove the rosemary sprigs and discard.

Preheat the oven to 200°C. Heat a baking tray at the same time.

Fill the pastry base with the cooled apple filling. Roll out the remaining dough to cover the top. Press the edges to seal with a fork and trim off any excess pastry. Brush the pastry with the egg and sprinkle on the sugar. Cut a hole in the top to allow the steam from the filling to escape. Slide the pie onto the heated baking tray and bake for 50 minutes to 1 hour until the pastry is crisp and golden.

Serves 6–8

1 egg, lightly beaten
coconut sugar, to sprinkle

PASTRY

250 g butter or ghee, chopped
350 g Italian 00 flour
1 tablespoon coconut sugar

FILLING

2 kg granny smith apples
2 tablespoons ghee
juice of 1 lemon
2 rosemary sprigs
1 vanilla pod, split and seeds scraped
pinch of saffron threads
1 teaspoon ground cinnamon
¼ cup (60 g) coconut sugar

Tahini and rose halva cookies

These chewy halva-like cookies are truly the business. A taste of these will transport you to Turkey or Morocco or somewhere in the incredible Middle East. Tahini is not recommended for Pittas but halva is okay because the sweet cools the warming tahini down. Make a double batch. You'll thank me.

Preheat the oven to 180°C. Line two baking trays with baking paper.

Place the tahini, sugar, egg and rosewater in a bowl and mix well. Keep mixing until the mixture comes away from the side of the bowl and forms a ball.

Shape tablespoons of the mixture into balls, flatten slightly. Place on the lined trays and bake for 10 minutes, until golden and firm.

Makes 12

1 cup (250 g) hulled tahini

1 cup (250 g) coconut sugar

1 egg, lightly beaten

1 tablespoon rosewater

Golden milk

Put the milk, spices and ghee or oil into a saucepan and bring to a simmer over low–medium heat for 5–10 minutes. Remove from the heat, stir in the syrup or sugar and set aside to infuse if you want a strong flavour. Alternatively, drink immediately.

Leftover golden milk can be stored in a glass bottle in the refrigerator for up to 5 days.

Serves 4

4 cups (1 litre) unhomogenised cow's milk or milk of your choice

1 tablespoon grated fresh turmeric or 1 heaped teaspoon ground turmeric

1 teaspoon ground cinnamon

1 teaspoon ghee or extra-virgin coconut oil

maple syrup or coconut sugar, to taste

Coconut kale crisps

Preheat the oven to 170°C. Line a large baking tray with baking paper.

Place the kale in a bowl and massage lightly to soften the leaves. Add the tamari, lemon juice and oil and mix well to coat the kale.

Spread the kale on the lined tray and bake for 15 minutes, checking a few times to make sure it doesn't burn. You want the kale to be crisp but not too dark or it will taste bitter.

Serves 4

1 bunch of kale (300 g), central stems removed, leaves torn into large bite-sized pieces

1 tablespoon tamari

1 tablespoon lemon juice

2 tablespoons melted extra-virgin coconut oil

Coconut custard with pomegranate and sticky rice

Normally, sticky rice is steamed but in this recipe I've cooked it just like other rice. It does take a little longer than other rice but, believe me, it is worth it. Standing the rice in cold water overnight reduces the cooking time.

Soak the sticky rice in cold water overnight; drain well.

Place the rice and lemongrass in a saucepan with 3 cups of water and bring to the boil. Cook over medium–high heat for 40 minutes, until the rice is soft and all the liquid has evaporated. Remove from the heat and allow to stand while you prepare the custard.

Place the coconut cream and kaffir lime leaves in a saucepan and bring to a simmer. Whisk together the cornflour or rice flour and 3 tablespoons of water until smooth, then stir into the coconut cream mixture and continue to stir until the mixture thickens.

Serve bowls of the coconut cream topped with the sticky rice and finish with the pomegranate seeds and a drizzle of maple syrup.

Serves 4

1 cup (200 g) white or black sticky rice
1 lemongrass stem, pale part only, bruised
2 cups (500 ml) coconut cream
6 kaffir lime leaves, bruised
1 tablespoon cornflour or rice flour
1 pomegranate, seeds removed
maple syrup, to serve

Vegan turmeric spiced banana loaf

This loaf is an absolute winner. It is delicious on its own topped with whatever tickles your fancy. And yes, it doesn't have any eggs. I've not made a mistake.

Preheat the oven to 180°C. Grease and line the base and sides of a 20 cm x 10 cm loaf tin with baking paper.

Place the almond meal, coconut, coconut sugar and chia seeds in a bowl. Add the spices and baking powder, then mix to combine.

Fold the banana and milk into the almond meal mixture, and set aside for 5 minutes.

Spoon the banana mixture into the prepared tin and bake for 40–50 minutes, until a skewer inserted in the centre of the loaf comes out clean. Allow to stand in the tin for 10 minutes before turning out onto a wire rack to cool completely before slicing. This is a moist loaf and might crumble a little when sliced.

Serves 6–8

1 cup (100 g) almond meal

1 cup (90 g) desiccated coconut

½ cup (90 g) coconut sugar

3 tablespoons chia seeds

3 teaspoons freshly grated nutmeg

1 teaspoon ground cardamom

1 teaspoon ground cinnamon

1 teaspoon ground turmeric

2 teaspoons baking powder

1 cup (240 g) mashed ripe sugar banana

1 cup (250 ml) coconut water or milk of your choice

Blueberry chia jam with fermented teff crepes

The batter will take longer to ferment on cooler days. The jam will last a month in the fridge.

For the crepes, whisk together the flour and water, cover and set aside for 2–4 days or until the mixture is sour and bubbling. Add salt and cinnamon to batter.

For the jam, place the blueberries in a bowl and mash lightly to break up the berries. Transfer the berries to a small saucepan, add the chia seeds, apple juice and zest and cook over medium heat for 10 minutes, until the mixture thickens. Spoon into clean dry jars, seal and cool. Refrigerate until ready to use.

Heat a little of the ghee in a 20 cm frypan, add ¼ cup of the batter to the pan and swirl to coat the base of the pan, pouring off any excess mixture. Cook for 2 minutes or until the crepe starts to leave the side of the pan. Turn and cook the other side for 1 minute. Keep warm while you cook the remaining batter. Spread a little of the chia jam onto the crepes and roll up to enclose.

Serves 4

CREPES

2 cups (200 g) teff flour

2¼ cups water

sea salt

1 teaspoon cinnamon

1 tablespoon ghee

JAM

2 cups (200 g) frozen blueberries, thawed

1 cup (160 g) chia seeds

1 cup (250 ml) apple juice

zest of 1 lemon

Kapha Recipes

LATE WINTER AND SPRING KAPHA SEASON

Kapha types will be more vulnerable to the elements in late winter and spring, as these are times when you become exposed to cool and damp conditions.

You will do well to stay warm at this time of year, and increase the amount of ginger, black pepper, cloves, cinnamon and cardamom you add to foods. Astringent foods will help too.

All doshas will benefit from following a Kapha diet in spring, as we all tend to eat heavier and moister foods in winter, which makes us more susceptible to colds.

Of all the doshas, it is Kapha who have the slowest metabolism. Yep, that's right. And that's why you don't eat much yet can't seem to lose weight. Kapha time is between 6–10 am, so this is when the dosha is most likely to become unbalanced. Skipping breakfast is a good option for you when you are feeling sluggish. Alternatively, you could choose to have a drink for breakfast.

Breakfast

Pomegranate and berry chia puddings

Chia seeds soak up moisture so they are great for Kapha types who can suffer from fluid retention, especially in spring or in the morning.

Place the chia gel ingredients in a saucepan, add 1 cup of water and mix to combine. Cook over low heat until the mixture thickens.

Spoon a layer of the berry puree into the bottom of four glasses, top with half the chia gel, add another layer of berry puree, then arrange the blueberries around the edge of the glass so you end up with a pretty layered pattern. Finish with the remaining chia gel. Cover and chill in the refrigerator for 4 hours until set.

Top the puddings with the coconut yoghurt and serve.

Serves 4

Berry Puree (page 76)
100 g fresh blueberries

CHIA GEL

½ cup (155 g) black chia seeds
1 cup (250 ml) apple juice
1 cup (250 ml) pomegranate juice

TOPPING

⅓ cup (80 g) coconut yoghurt

Spiced puffed grain granola

You may wonder why I have not tossed the cereal in the honey and then baked it. In Ayurveda we do not heat honey, as it is said to create a build-up of ama (toxins) in the digestive tract. Enjoy your cereal with warm milk – all types of milk are hard to digest and even more so when they are cold. Your best choices are goat's or cow's milk, rice milk or almond milk, in that order.

Preheat the oven to 180°C. Line two large baking trays with baking paper.

Place the puffed grains in a large bowl, add the spices, coconut and seeds and mix to combine. Add the oil and mix until the grains are coated. Spread the granola mixture on the prepared trays and bake, stirring occasionally to cook evenly, for 5–10 minutes, until crisp and golden.

Remove the granola from the oven and pour in the honey, mix quickly to coat. Cool on the trays before stirring in the cherries or cranberries, apricots and goji berries.

Tip the granola into an airtight container and store for up to 3 weeks.

Makes 12 cups

3 cups (55 g) puffed corn
3 cups (120 g) puffed amaranth
3 cups (120 g) puffed millet
1 teaspoon ground cinnamon
1 teaspoon ground turmeric
½ cup (30 g) shredded coconut
½ cup (60 g) sunflower seeds
½ cup (70 g) pumpkin seed kernels (pepitas)
½ cup (125 ml) almond or sunflower oil
2 tablespoons raw honey
½ cup (100 g) dried sour cherries or cranberries, chopped
½ cup (90 g) dried apricots, chopped
½ cup (50 g) goji berries

Turmeric tofu scramble with leafy greens

Tofu is cooling and heavy, so it should be eaten in moderation by Kapha individuals. In this recipe I have made it more digestible by warming it and adding spices. Serve this as part of a nourishing bowl for breakfast, lunch or dinner. Team it with some steamed greens, sprouts, fried mushrooms, sauerkraut or pickled vegetables and serve on top of quinoa or buckwheat.

You could add miso instead of the spices if you like to have tofu for breakfast and want to mix things up.

Heat half the oil in a frying pan, add the spring onion and brussels sprouts and cook for 5 minutes or until the sprouts are golden. Add the spices and cook over medium heat until the spices are fragrant, 3 minutes. Add the tofu and cook for 5 minutes, until it is warmed through.

Pour the remaining oil into the pan, add the nutritional yeast and ginger and cook for 1 minute. Throw the kale into the pan with a splash of water and cook, stirring, until the leaves are just wilted and the water evaporates.

Serve the leaves topped with the tofu scramble, the sprouts and pickled vegetables.

Serves 4

1 tablespoon mustard or sunflower oil

2 spring onions, sliced

200 g brussels sprouts, thinly sliced

½ teaspoon ground turmeric

½ teaspoon sweet paprika

1 teaspoon ground cumin

½ teaspoon ground cinnamon

300 g medium-firm tofu, crumbled into large pieces

2 teaspoons nutritional yeast

1 tablespoon grated ginger

1 bunch of kale (about 300 g), central stems removed, leaves roughly chopped

3 tablespoons finely shredded pickled cabbage and beetroot

Ginger, apple, cinnamon and clove tea

Place the apple, ginger, cinnamon and cloves in a saucepan with 1.25 litres of water and bring to the boil. Reduce the heat and simmer for 20 minutes, until the tea turns a light golden colour and the apple begins to soften.

Ladle the tea into mugs, add a slice or two of apple and serve.

1 apple, cut crossways into 1 cm thick slices

1 tablespoon thinly sliced ginger

1 cinnamon stick

4 cloves

Breakfast drinks and smoothies

When making any of these drinks keep in mind that your constitution is already cold, so drinking an iced juice or smoothie from 6–10 in the morning is not the smartest choice for you to be making on cold days. Of all the things I recommend to my Kapha clients, the suggestion that skipping breakfast is okay has been the most life changing. For years now our society has rammed down our throats the importance of breakfast, but there is no one-size-fits-all approach to health and wellness. If you are not hungry, then start your day with some hot lemon and water or a green smoothie.

Winter green smoothie

Place the celery, spinach, coconut water and 1 cup of water in a high-speed blender; blend until smooth.

Add the pear or apple, dates, avocado, ginger and chia seeds; blend again until smooth and creamy.

Serves 2

1 small celery stalk, chopped
2 cups (50 g) trimmed and chopped English spinach leaves
1 cup (250 ml) coconut water
1 small pear or apple, cored and chopped
2 medjool dates, pitted
½ avocado, sliced
2 teaspoons finely grated ginger
1 tablespoon white chia seeds

Berry blush smoothie

Place the berries, cardamom, chia seeds, honey, milk and 1 cup of water in a high-speed blender and blend until smooth and creamy.

Serves 2

1 cup (220 g) mixed fresh berries
½ teaspoon ground cardamom
1 tablespoon chia seeds
1 teaspoon raw honey
1 cup (250 ml) soy milk or almond milk

Carrot, celery, ginger and raspberry juice for spring

Push the carrots, celery, ginger and raspberries through a juicer.

Serves 2

4 carrots, roughly chopped
2 celery stalks, roughly chopped
a thumb-sized piece of ginger
50 g fresh raspberries

Turmeric energy smoothie

This is a really different smoothie that ticks a lot of boxes for me. Again, I like that it is not sweetened with banana, as banana can aggravate the Kapha dosha, especially in the colder months.

Place the raisins, dates, prunes, spices, milk and 1 cup of water in a high-speed blender and blend until smooth and creamy.

Serves 2

1 tablespoon raisins
2 medjool dates, pitted
2 prunes, pitted
½ teaspoon ground turmeric
½ teaspoon ground cinnamon
freshly ground black pepper
1 cup (250 ml) soy milk or almond milk

Buckwheat and beetroot pancakes with berries

I wanted to make a pancake that was Kapha-friendly, so free of egg, almond meal and banana.

Sift the flours, baking powder and cinnamon into a bowl. Stir in the beetroot and sugar and make a well in the centre.

Whisk together the chia seeds and milk.

Add the wet ingredients to the dry ingredients and mix to combine. Allow to stand for 5–10 minutes to thicken slightly. You want the batter to be a thin pouring consistency, not thick, or the pancakes will be stodgy.

Heat a little of the ghee in a large non-stick frying pan over medium heat, add 3 tablespoons of batter per pancake to the pan and cook four at a time. Cook until bubbles appear on the surface, about 3 minutes, then turn and cook on the other side for 2 minutes. Transfer to a plate and keep warm. Repeat with the remaining batter until you have ten pancakes in total.

Serve the pancakes topped with the raspberries and drizzled with the honey.

1 cup (130 g) buckwheat flour

¼ cup (65 g) coconut flour

1 teaspoon baking powder

1 teaspoon ground cinnamon

½ cup (120 g) grated beetroot (about 1 beetroot)

1 tablespoon coconut sugar

1 tablespoon chia seeds

2 cups (500 ml) soy milk (or Kapha-suitable milk)

2 tablespoons ghee

150 g raspberries

2 tablespoons raw honey

Serves 4–6

Mushrooms and kale with millet and goat's cheese

You can use quinoa instead of millet if you haven't had time to soak the millet or don't have any in your cupboard.

Rinse and drain the millet.

Place the millet and shiitake mushrooms in a pan with 3 cups of water and bring to the boil. Cook over medium–high heat for 20 minutes, until the millet is soft, and then drain well.

Melt the ghee in a large frying pan, add the garlic and spring onion and cook over medium heat for 5 minutes, until the spring onion is soft. Add the mixed mushrooms, increase the heat to high and cook until they are soft and browned.

Add the millet and kale to the pan and gently mix to combine. Season with salt and pepper.

Divide the mushrooms, kale and millet between serving bowls, add a big squeeze of lemon juice and serve topped with the goat's cheese.

1 cup (190 g) millet, soaked overnight in cold water

3 tablespoons dried shiitake mushrooms

3 tablespoons ghee

1 garlic clove, chopped

2 spring onions, sliced

500 g mixed mushrooms (such as shimeji, enoki, Swiss brown)

2 cups (150 g) roughly chopped and steamed kale

sea salt and freshly ground black pepper

1 lemon, halved

100 g goat's cheese

Serves 4

Shakshuka with lentils

You will notice I have used beans with yoghurt in this recipe. To remedy this incompatible food combination, I have added digestive spices to the yoghurt.

Heat the oil in a large frying pan, add the onion and cook, stirring occasionally, over medium heat for 10 minutes, until the onion is soft and golden. Add the paprika and cook, stirring, for 1 minute until fragrant. Stir in the tomatoes, capsicum and lentils and season to taste. Bring to the boil, reduce the heat and simmer for 20 minutes, until the sauce has thickened.

Use a large spoon to make eight indentations in the sauce. Crack in the eggs, one by one, cover and cook over medium heat for 10 minutes, until the eggs are cooked to your liking.

Put the yoghurt into a bowl, add 1 tablespoon of water.

Smash the cumin, fennel and 1 teaspoon of salt together in a mortar and pestle.

Top the shakshuka with the fennel spice, yoghurt and parsley.

1 tablespoon sunflower oil

1 red onion, finely chopped

1 teaspoon smoked paprika

2 x 400 g cans diced tomatoes

250 g bottled roasted red capsicum, sliced

1 x 400 g can lentils, rinsed and drained

sea salt and freshly ground black pepper

8 eggs

⅓ cup (90 g) Greek-style yoghurt

2 teaspoons cumin seeds

2 teaspoons fennel seeds

2 tablespoons chopped fresh parsley

Serves 4

Buckwheat porridge with raspberry puree and pomegranate

Buckwheat is a drying grain, making it the perfect choice for Kapha types at breakfast. The morning is a time when you may feel more mucousy or heavy in the chest. Teaming the porridge with pomegranate, which is astringent and drying, is a fabulous way to absorb some of the moisture.

Place the buckwheat in a non-metallic bowl, cover with warm water and add the vinegar. Cover and allow to rest overnight. Drain and rinse until the water runs clean.

Place the raspberries and maple syrup in a high-speed blender and blend until they are smooth. Remove ½ cup of puree and set aside.

Add the drained buckwheat to the remaining raspberry puree in the blender, add the milk or water, banana, rosewater and vanilla and blend until smooth and creamy.

Layer the blended buckwheat mixture with the reserved raspberry puree and the pomegranate seeds in serving bowls. Finish with the pomegranate seeds and a drizzle of maple syrup.

1 cup (195 g) buckwheat

1 tablespoon apple cider vinegar

250 g fresh raspberries

1 tablespoon pure maple syrup, plus extra to serve

½ cup (125 ml) soy or rice milk or water

1 banana, chopped

1 teaspoon rosewater

1 teaspoon vanilla powder or natural vanilla extract

¼ cup (30 g) pomegranate seeds

Serves 4

Cauliflower bean puree with watercress, mushrooms and poached eggs

This cauliflower bean puree is a wonderful alternative to teaming your breakfast with toast. If you do eat bread, try to make it sourdough, which is easier for Kaphas' sluggish digestion to cope with.

Preheat the grill to high. Place the cauliflower in a saucepan with the ghee, beans, stock and ½ cup of water and bring to the boil. Reduce the heat to low and simmer, covered, for 20 minutes, until the cauliflower is very soft.

Puree the mixture with a hand-held blender until smooth. Season with salt and pepper.

Place the mushrooms onto a baking tray lined with baking paper. Brush the mushrooms with the melted ghee, and grill the mushrooms until golden brown.

Poach the eggs in a frying pan of simmering water until cooked to your liking, and drain well.

Serve the cauliflower puree topped with the peppercorns, watercress, mushrooms and poached eggs.

2 cups (250 g) chopped cauliflower (about ½ small cauliflower)

2 tablespoons ghee

1 x 400 g can cannellini beans, rinsed and drained

1 cup (250 ml) homemade Vegetable or Chicken Stock (pages 220 and 224)

sea salt and pink, green and black peppercorns

1 bunch watercress

8 field mushrooms

1 tablespoon ghee, melted

8 eggs

Matcha polenta porridge

Matcha is powdered green tea. It has a strong distinct flavour and can be used in porridge, pancake batter and warm milk. It's not cheap so store in an airtight container.

Heat the milk, 1 cup of water and the matcha powder in a saucepan. Bring to the boil and add the polenta in a thin steady stream, stirring with a whisk until the porridge thickens. Change to a wooden spoon and cook, stirring, for 5 minutes, until the porridge starts to come away from the side of the pan. Remove from the heat and sweeten with the vanilla and maple syrup.

Top the porridge with the pumpkin seeds and sesame seeds and a drizzle of maple syrup.

Serves 4

2 cups (500 ml) milk of your choice (goat's, cow's, rice, soy or almond are best for Kaphas)

2 teaspoons matcha powder

1 cup (190 g) instant polenta

1 teaspoon vanilla powder or natural vanilla extract

1 tablespoon maple syrup

2 tablespoons pumpkin seeds

2 teaspoons black sesame seeds

Corn 3 ways

CORN AND DILL FRITTERS

Place the corn, spring onion and dill in a bowl and mix to combine.

Whisk together the eggs and flour until smooth. Combine with corn mix.

Heat the oil in a non-stick frying pan, add 2 tablespoons of batter per fritter to the pan and cook, in batches of three, over medium heat until bubbles appear on the surface. Turn and cook on the other side for 3 minutes, until the fritters are cooked through. Transfer to a plate and keep warm. Repeat with the remaining mixture until you have eight fritters in total. Serve with lime slices.

Serves 4

2 cups (400 g) corn kernels

2 spring onions, chopped

2 tablespoons chopped dill

2 eggs

2 tablespoons buckwheat flour or cornflour

2 tablespoons sunflower oil

1 lime, sliced

GARLIC CORN COBS

Place the corn, lemon juice and kaffir lime leaves in a saucepan of boiling water and cook over high heat for 15 minutes, until the corn is tender. Drain well.

Combine the ghee and garlic, rub over the corn and serve hot.

Serves 2–4

4 corn cobs

juice of 1 lemon

4 kaffir lime leaves

1 tablespoon ghee

1 garlic clove, finely grated

SWEET HONEY CORN POLENTA PORRIDGE

Place the milk, vanilla, cinnamon and 1 cup of water in a saucepan and bring to the boil. Gradually whisk in the polenta, then change to a wooden spoon and cook, stirring constantly. Add corn after polenta thickens and softens.

Serve the polenta topped with the yoghurt and berries and drizzled with the maple syrup.

Serves 4

1 cup (250 ml) soy milk

1 teaspoon vanilla powder

1 teaspoon ground cinnamon

1 cup (190 g) instant polenta

1 cup (200 g) corn kernels

2 tablespoons yoghurt

200 g fresh berries

1 tablespoon honey

Lunch

Rocket, pear and quickled onion and radish salad

There is a bit of fiddling around as you need to pickle vegies but after that you are pretty much done.

To make the quickled onion and radish, place the red onion, radish, vinegar, spices, honey and ½ cup of water in a bowl and mix to combine. Allow to stand for as long as time permits.

Rinse the quinoa under cold running water, then drain. Cook the quinoa in boiling water for 15 minutes, until the tails start to separate from the grain. Rinse under cold water and drain well.

Arrange the greens, quinoa and pear on a serving plate, and top with some of the drained quickled onion and radish.

Combine the dressing ingredients in a bowl, add 1 tablespoon of quickled onion and radish liquid and whisk together.

Drizzle the dressing over the salad, scatter on the goat's cheese and pomegranate seeds and serve topped with the grated hard boiled egg.

Serves 4

⅓ cup (65 g) quinoa

150 g wild rocket leaves or leafy greens

2 pears, thinly sliced on a mandoline

100 g goat's cheese

seeds of 1 pomegranate

4 hard-boiled eggs, peeled

QUICKLED ONION AND RADISH

1 small red onion, thinly sliced on a mandoline

1 bunch of radishes, thinly sliced on a mandoline

1 cup (250 ml) apple cider vinegar

1 teaspoon each of mustard seeds, dill seeds and juniper berries

2 teaspoons raw honey

DRESSING

1 tablespoon apple juice

2 tablespoons extra-virgin olive oil

Sweet beet and cabbage with fish steaks

This beet and cabbage could be served as a side to roasted meats or as a warm salad. The addition of the smoked trout makes it a tasty lunch. It can be served hot or cold.

Warm the cauliflower puree in a pan and set aside.

Heat the oil in a large saucepan, add the cabbage and a splash of water and cook over medium heat for 5 minutes, until the cabbage is soft. Add the beetroot and cook for 2 minutes.

Heat the oil in a large frypan, over a medium high heat, add the fish and cook for 5 minutes each side or until tender.

Whisk together the sesame seeds, maple syrup and balsamic vinegar. Add to the pan and cook for 5 minutes, until the cabbage and beetroot are warmed through and most of the liquid has been absorbed.

Serve the cauliflower puree, topped with cabbage and beetroot and the fish and a sprig of dill and cornichons.

Serves 4

Cauliflower puree, page 175

1 tablespoon organic sesame oil

¼ red cabbage, finely shredded

1 small beetroot, grated

1 tablespoon olive oil

4 x 125 g pieces white fish – marlin, snapper, mahi mahi

2 tablespoons sesame seeds, toasted

1 tablespoon pure maple syrup

2 tablespoons balsamic vinegar

6 dill fronds

20 cornichons

Carrot, basil and buckwheat bread

I've based this recipe on Jacqueline Alwill's tried and tested one from her *The Brown Paper Bag* website. Serve with blueberry chia jam (page 160), a little ghee or smokey hummus and homemade chutney.

Place the buckwheat and seeds into a bowl, cover with cold water and leave to soak overnight. The next morning, rinse under cold water and drain well. I allow at least 15 minutes for them to drain.

Preheat the oven to 160°C. Grease and line the base and sides of a 21 cm x 11 cm loaf tin.

Place the chia seeds in a bowl, add 1 cup of water and set aside for 10 minutes to form a gel.

Put the buckwheat and seeds into a bowl, add the chia gel, yeast, psyllium, ghee, turmeric, carrot, basil and salt. Spoon the mixture into the prepared tin and smooth the top. Cover with a tea towel and sit for 2 hours. Bake for 1½ hours until a skewer inserted in the centre comes out clean. Check after an hour or so and cover with foil if the top is browning too quickly. The outside will be crisp long before the centre is cooked. Cool in the tin for 30 minutes before turning out onto a wire rack to cool completely.

Serves 6

1¾ cups (350 g) buckwheat

1 cup (200 g) mixed sunflower and pumpkin seeds

½ cup (80 g) black chia seeds

1 tablespoon nutrional yeast

4 tablespoons psyllium husk

2 tablespoons ghee

1 tablespoon grated fresh turmeric

2 cups (310 g) grated carrot

3 tablespoons shredded basil

sea salt

Buckwheat, cranberry, tomato and pomegranate tabouleh

This version of tabouleh uses buckwheat instead of the traditional cracked wheat. Wheat is the heaviest and most moist of all grains, which makes it unsuitable for Kaphas.

Rinse the buckwheat and drain well, then place in a saucepan, add 2 cups of water and bring to the boil. Continue to boil for 15 minutes, until the buckwheat is just soft. Remove from the heat and rinse under cold water. Drain well.

Transfer the buckwheat to a bowl, add the herbs, tomato, cranberries and pomegranate seeds and mix to combine.

Whisk together the dressing ingredients, pour over the salad and toss to coat.

Serves 4

½ cup (100 g) buckwheat, soaked in cold water overnight

1 cup (20g) each of chopped flat-leaf parsley, chopped basil and chopped dill

200 g cherry tomatoes, roughly chopped

⅓ cup (40 g) dried cranberries

3 tablespoons pomegranate seeds

DRESSING

2 tablespoons extra-virgin olive oil

2 tablespoons lemon juice

1 garlic clove, crushed

1 teaspoon dill seeds, lightly crushed

Beetroot and black bean burgers

My gorgeous friend Lucy asked me to write a recipe for these as she had been buying something similar from the supermarket. Challenge accepted and completed, and I'm thrilled with the end result. They are surprisingly tasty for something with such a limited amount of ingredients. I didn't chill them for very long when I tested the recipe and they still stuck together. Make sure you mash half the beans and the buckwheat, as this helps bind the burgers.

These are great with just a squeeze of lime, but if you want something a bit more, you could serve them with a herbed yoghurt if you, like me, enjoy a condiment.

Kaphas, these are a better choice for you than a veg burger that is based on higher carb vegetables like sweet potato or pumpkin, which you need to limit, especially in spring and winter when you probably crave them.

Place the black beans, onion, beetroot, pumpkin seeds, buckwheat and nutritional yeast in a bowl and mix to combine. Shape the mixture into six even-sized patties and place on a tray lined with baking paper. Chill in the fridge for 2 hours, or overnight if time permits.

Heat the oil in a frying pan over medium–high heat, add the patties in batches of two and cook for 7 minutes on each side until browned and heated through. Transfer to a warm plate.

Serve the burgers inside warm blue corn tortillas with cos lettuce leaves and a good dollop of yoghurt with a big squeeze of lime.

Makes 6

1 x 400 g can black beans, rinsed and drained and roughly mashed

1 onion, grated

1 cup (140 g) grated beetroot

2 tablespoons pumpkin seeds, roughly chopped

½ cup (100 g) cooked buckwheat, roughly mashed

2 tablespoons nutritional yeast

sunflower or extra-virgin coconut oil, for frying

6 blue corn tortillas

1 baby cos lettuce, leaves seperated

½ cup (125 g) Greek style yoghurt

1 lime, halved

Split pea and leek soup with minty basil yoghurt swirl

This is the healthy cousin of pea 'n' ham soup, which I absolutely adore but can't eat too much of these days.

Heat the oil in a large saucepan, add the leek and cook, stirring occasionally, over medium heat for 10 minutes, until soft but not browned. Stir in the celery and carrot and cook for 5 minutes, until they are soft. Add the bay leaf, peppercorns, split peas, stock and mint and bring to the boil. Reduce the heat to low and simmer for 2 hours until the split peas are very soft. Blend with a hand-held blender until smooth. Season with salt and pepper.

Place the minty basil yoghurt ingredients in a blender, add ½ cup of water and blend until smooth.

Serve bowls of the soup, topped with a swirl of the minty basil yoghurt. Sprinkle with the chilli, if desired, and serve.

Serves 4–6

2 tablespoons sunflower oil

1 leek, white part only, thinly sliced

2 celery stalks, chopped

1 carrot, chopped

1 bay leaf

4 black peppercorns

500 g green split peas, soaked in cold water overnight

1.5–2 litres homemade Chicken Stock (page 220)

2 mint sprigs

sea salt and freshly ground black pepper

chilli flakes, to serve (optional)

MINTY BASIL YOGHURT

1 cup (250 g) Greek-style yoghurt

2 garlic cloves, crushed

1 cup (20 g) basil leaves

1 cup (20 g) mint leaves

Charred cauliflower and broccoli with turmeric quinoa

Preheat the barbecue to hot.

Rinse the quinoa, transfer to a saucepan of boiling water, add the turmeric and pepper and cook for 15 minutes, until the tails start to separate from the grain. Drain well and set aside to cool.

Brush the oil on the barbecue flat plate, add the cauliflower and broccoli steaks and cook for 15 minutes, turning a few times, until the cauliflower and broccoli are charred and tender.

Arrange the quinoa on a plate, top with the charred cauliflower and broccoli, and sprinkle on the pumpkin seeds over the top.

Whisk the dressing ingredients with 2–3 tablespoons of water until you have a smooth thin dressing. Add a little more water if it is too thick.

Drizzle the dressing over the salad and serve sprinkled with the pomegranate seeds.

Serves 4

½ cup (100 g) quinoa

½ teaspoon ground turmeric

½ teaspoon freshly ground black pepper

2 tablespoons olive oil

1 small head of cauliflower, cut into 4 x 3 cm thick steaks

1 small head of broccoli, cut into 4 x 3 cm thick steaks

2 tablespoons pumpkin seeds

2 tablespoons pomegranate seeds

DRESSING

2 tablespoons hulled tahini

2 tablespoons coconut yoghurt

2 teaspoons dijon mustard

1 tablespoon lemon juice

Broad bean, chicken and crunchy green salad

This is a great spring or summer salad. I know peeling broad beans is time-consuming but going to the extra effort is so worth it.

Heat the olive oil in a saucepan, add the onion and cook over medium heat for 10 minutes, until the onion is soft but not coloured. Add the broad beans and peas and cook for 5 minutes, until heated through. Remove from the heat and allow to cool.

Add the lettuce, sprouts and dill to the pan, and gently mix to combine.

Pile the salad onto plates and top with the chicken.

Whisk together the dressing ingredients, add 2 tablespoons of water and whisk until you have a thin dressing.

Drizzle the dressing over the salad and serve.

Serves 4

2 tablespoons olive oil

1 onion, finely chopped

500 g frozen broad beans, thawed and peeled

1 cup (130 g) frozen baby peas

2 cups (130 g) torn crisp lettuce (such as cos)

1 cup (130 g) sunflower sprouts

3 tablespoons chopped fresh dill

2 chicken breast fillets, poached and shredded

DRESSING

1 tablespoon dijon mustard

1 teaspoon grated fresh horseradish or horseradish cream

1 tablespoon lemon juice

1 garlic clove, crushed

1 tablespoon mustard oil

pinch of sea salt

Cauliflower 3 ways

CAULIFLOWER WITH MUSTARD SEEDS AND POMEGRANATE

Preheat oven to 200°C. Line a baking tray with baking paper. Place the cauliflower onto the tray, sprinkle with mustard seeds and turmeric and drizzle with oil. Roast for 40 minutes or until the cauliflower starts to blacken. Transfer to a plate, squeeze over the lemon, scatter over the pomegranate seeds and parsley and serve.

Serves 2–4

300 g cauliflower, cut into florets
1 tablespoon sunflower oil
1 teaspoon black mustard seeds
½ teaspoon ground turmeric
juice of 1 lemon
2 tablespoons pomegranate seeds
a handful of torn flat-leaf parsley

MISO CAULIFLOWER

Preheat the oven to 180°C. Line a baking tray with baking paper.

Place the cauliflower on the lined tray.

Put the miso, mustard, mirin, tamari, sesame seeds and 2 tablespoons of water into a saucepan and cook, stirring occasionally, over medium heat without boiling for about 5 minutes, until smooth.

Spoon half the miso mixture over the cauliflower. Bake for 30 minutes, spoon the remaining mixture over and bake for 30 minutes more or until the cauliflower is tender.

Serves 4–6

1 head of cauliflower, leaves trimmed
2 tablespoons shiro miso
1 tablespoon wholegrain mustard
1 tablespoon mirin
1 tablespoon tamari
2 teaspoons black sesame seeds

SPICED CAULIFLOWER RICE

This is a great alternative to rice (which is cooling and can aggravate Kaphas if eaten too often). Serve with curries or stir-fries.

Finely chop the cauliflower in a food processor until it resembles pieces of rice.

Steam the cauliflower, ginger and cumin seeds in a fine colander set over a saucepan of boiling water for 10 minutes, until the cauliflower is soft. Stir through the ghee, zest and lemon juice and serve.

Serves 4

1 head of cauliflower, roughly chopped
1 tablespoon finely shredded ginger
1 teaspoon cumin seeds
1 tablespoon ghee
zest and juice of 1 lemon

Dinner

Slow-cooked Mediterranean green beans and fennel with buckwheat

This dish is fabulous as a stand-alone vegetarian meal or it can be served with fish, chicken or turkey, which are the most suited animal foods for Kaphas.

Preheat the oven to 150°C.

Layer the beans, fennel and onion in an ovenproof dish, top with the tomatoes, oregano, oil and 400 ml of water and season with pinch of salt and a good grinding of pepper. Cover the surface with baking paper cut to fit (a cartouche) and bake for 2 hours.

Rinse the buckwheat and drain. Cook the buckwheat in a saucepan of boiling water for 15 minutes, until just soft. Drain well.

Serve the buckwheat with the slow-cooked beans and fennel.

Serves 4–6

300 g green beans, topped and tailed

1 fennel bulb, sliced

1 onion, sliced

1 x 400 g can diced tomatoes

3 sprigs fresh oregano

3 tablespoons olive oil

sea salt and freshly ground black pepper

1 cup (195 g) buckwheat, soaked for 2 hours in cold water

Middle Eastern eggplant and red capsicum salad

Preheat a barbecue chargrill plate. Brush the eggplant lightly with oil and chargrill the eggplant slices and whole red capsicum until the eggplant slices are soft and golden and the red capsicum is blistered and blackened all over. Allow the red capsicum to cool and then peel away the blackened skin. Tear the flesh into strips.

Arrange the spinach leaves on top of a serving plate, top with eggplant and red capsicum pieces, and drizzle with the olive oil and pomegranate molasses.

Serves 4 as a side

1 large eggplant, cut into thick slices

2 red capsicum

2 tablespoons olive oil

2 handfuls spinach leaves

olive oil, to drizzle

pomegranate molasses, to drizzle

Fish tacos

Fish tacos make a quick evening meal or a fab dinner when you are entertaining; simply place everything on the table and let guests serve themselves.

I love using blue corn tortillas as they are more warming and better for Kaphas than wheat flour ones.

Place the fish fillets in a shallow dish, sprinkle both sides with the cumin, paprika and a pinch of salt and drizzle on the oil.

Heat the barbecue to medium–hot. Cook the fish on the barbecue for 5 minutes on each side until just cooked.

Place the cabbage, coriander and lime juice in a bowl and use your hands to combine, squeezing the cabbage to release any juice.

Combine the avocado sauce ingredients in a small blender and blend until smooth.

Warm the tortillas on the barbecue for 1–2 minutes on each side. Fill the tortillas with the fish, cabbage salad and avocado sauce and serve.

Serves 4

4 fish fillets, pin-boned – firm white fish: kingfish, marlin, mackerel

1 teaspoon ground cumin

1 teaspoon smoked sweet paprika

sea salt

1 tablespoon olive oil

2 cups (150 g) finely shredded savoy cabbage

½ cup (10 g) coriander leaves

lime juice

8 corn tortillas

AVOCADO SAUCE

1 tablespoon mayonnaise (I love Kewpie mayo)

1 avocado, halved and flesh removed

1 tablespoon lime juice

1 garlic clove, chopped

Eggplant curry

Cut the eggplant into bite-size cubes and place into a colander over a bowl. Sprinkle generously with the salt and set aside for 30 minutes for the salt to draw the moisture out of the eggplant. Rinse the salt off the eggplant and then pat the eggplant really dry using paper towel. This will stop it spitting in the oil.

Heat the oil in a large deep frypan over a medium–high heat. Add the eggplant in batches and cook for 5 minutes or until golden brown. Don't be tempted to rush this step, if you do your eggplant will be rubbery. Drain the cooked eggplant on absorbent paper.

Drain most of the oil from the pan, leaving only a couple of tablespoons, add the onion and cook over a medium heat for 10 minutes or until the onion is golden. Add the spices and cook for 2 minutes or until fragrant.

Stir in the tomato paste and water and bring to boil, add the eggplant, cover and cook for 15 minutes or until the sauce has thickened.

Serve with rice.

Serves 4

500 g eggplant

salt for sprinkling on the eggplant

⅓ cup (80 ml) sunflower oil

1 onion, finely chopped

1 teaspoon black mustard seeds

1 green chilli, chopped

1 tablespoon garlic ginger paste

½ teaspoon chilli powder, optional

1 teaspoon turmeric

1 teaspoon ground cumin

½ teaspoon garam marsala

1 tablespoon tomato paste

½ cup–1 cup (125 ml–250 ml) water

Rajasthani mixed lentil dhal

There are a few things that make a good dhal for me, and I think the most important is texture. I'm not a fan of watery dhals, I much prefer them rich and creamy – and this one truly is that. The secret is in cooking the dhal, you can't rush it. If you do, you are likely to find yourself with a pan with a nicely charred base; believe me, I've needed a lot of elbow grease to clean some of my rushed ventures. This one takes about 1½ hours if you cook it the old-fashioned way on the stove; if you prefer, you could use a pressure cooker or a slow cooker.

Place the urad and mung dhal in a bowl, cover with water and set aside to soak overnight. Rinse and drain well.

Transfer the dhal to a large saucepan, add 2 litres of water and cook over medium heat for 1½ hours, checking and stirring several times to see if you need to add more water. The dhal is ready when the mixture is thick and slightly creamy. You may need to increase the heat towards the end if you find there is too much liquid.

Add the chilli powder, turmeric and tamarind to the pan and mix to combine.

Heat the oil in a small saucepan, add the cloves and bay leaves and cook over medium heat for 1 minute, add the remaining spices and cook for 1 minute until fragrant. Add to the cooked lentil mixture and stir through.

Divide the dhal between serving bowls, top with the yoghurt, finish with a good squeeze of lemon and a sprinkle of coriander and mint leaves.

Serves 4

1 cup (250 g) urad dhal
1 cup (220 g) split mung dhal
½ teaspoon chilli powder
½ teaspoon ground turmeric
1 tablespoon tamarind puree
2 tablespoons organic sesame oil
3 cloves
2 dried bay leaves
1 teaspoon garam masala
1 teaspoon ground cumin
1 teaspoon ground coriander

To serve
½ cup (125 g) Greek style yoghurt
1 lemon, halved
coriander leaves
mint leaves

Asian noodle broth with chicken balls

Soak the noodles in hot water for 20 minutes while you prepare the soup.

Place the mince, egg white and coriander in a bowl, season with salt and pepper and mix to combine. Shape the mixture into walnut-sized balls.

Place the stock, sesame oil, tamari, ginger, garlic (if using) mushrooms and 2 cups (500 ml) water in a large saucepan and bring to a simmer. Add the meatballs and simmer for 10 minutes, skimming the surface to remove any scum that has gathered on top.

Once the meatballs are cooked, add the snow peas, broccolini, lotus root and cook for 5 minutes, until the vegetables are just tender. Divide the noodles between serving bowls and spoon over the meatballs, vegetables and broth.

Serves 4

100 g buckwheat noodles

250 g chicken, beef or pork mince

1 small egg white

a handful of chopped coriander

sea salt and freshly ground white pepper

4 cups (1 litre) homemade stock of your choice (pages 220–4)

1 teaspoon toasted sesame oil

1 tablespoon tamari

1 tablespoon sliced ginger

1 garlic clove, sliced (optional)

100 g Swiss brown mushrooms, sliced

50 g snow peas, trimmed

12 slices lotus root

1 bunch of broccolini, roughly chopped

Cauliflower and broccoli fried rice

Rice is considered to be cooling for Kaphas, so this is a great alternative if you like fried rice. If you don't have a food processor, you can grate the cauliflower and broccoli but watch your fingers.

Put the cauliflower and broccoli into a food processor and pulse until you have roughly rice-sized pieces.

Heat 1 teaspoon of coconut oil in a wok or large frying pan, add the egg and swirl to coat the base of the pan. Cook over medium heat until the edge and top are just set, about 3 minutes, then turn and cook the other side until set. Remove the omelette from the pan, allow to cool slightly, then cut into thin strips.

Heat the remaining coconut oil in the wok or pan, add the spring onion, ginger, celery and capsicum and stir-fry for 5 minutes, until the capsicum is softened. Add the cauliflower and broccoli mix, the peas, corn, stock, tamari and sesame oil and stir-fry for 5 minutes, until the cauliflower and broccoli are softened.

Remove the wok or pan from the heat, fold through the omelette, coriander and sesame seeds.

Serves 4

350 g cauliflower (about ½), cut into florets

250 g broccoli, cut into florets

2 tablespoons extra-virgin coconut oil

2 eggs, lightly beaten

2 spring onions, thinly sliced

1 tablespoon grated ginger

1 celery stalk, chopped

1 red capsicum, diced

½ cup (60 g) frozen baby peas, thawed

½ cup (100 g) corn kernels

½ cup (125 ml) homemade Chicken Stock (page 220)

1 tablespoon tamari

a few drops of toasted sesame oil

2 tablespoons chopped coriander

2 tablespoons sesame seeds, toasted

Turmeric 3 ways

TURMERIC CHICKEN SKEWERS

Serve with salad leaves and barbecued vegetables.

Place the chicken in a bowl, add the spices, fish sauce, lime juice, sugar and 2 tablespoons of water and mix to combine. Cover and marinate for as long as time permits.

Soak eight rosemary skewers in cold water for 20 minutes.

Heat the barbecue to medium–hot.

Thread the chicken onto fresh rosemary skewers. Cook on the barbecue flat plate, turning several times, for 15 minutes, until the chicken is cooked through and tender.

Serves 4

8 fresh rosemary sprigs, made into skewers by removing the bottom leaves
500 g chicken breast fillets, thinly sliced
1 teaspoon ground turmeric
1 teaspoon curry powder
1 tablespoon grated ginger
1 tablespoon fish sauce
1 tablespoon lime juice
1 teaspoon coconut sugar

TURMERIC FIG SHAKE

Place the spices and vanilla in a blender, add the figs, chia seeds, coconut milk and 1 cup of water and blend until smooth.

Serves 2

1 teaspoon ground turmeric
½ teaspoon ground cinnamon
½ teaspoon vanilla powder
2 soft dried figs
1 tablespoon chia seeds
1 cup (250 ml) light coconut milk

TURMERIC CARROT BUCKWHEAT PORRIDGE

Put the buckwheat, carrot, coconut milk, 1 cup of water and the spices into a saucepan and cook over medium heat for 10 minutes, until the carrot is soft. Spoon the porridge into bowls, top with a little extra coconut milk, the dried fruit and a drizzle of honey.

Serves 4

1 cup (250 g) cooked buckwheat
2 cups (200 g) grated carrot
1 cup (250 ml) coconut milk, plus extra to serve
1 teaspoon ground turmeric
½ teaspoon ground cardamom
½ teaspoon ground ginger
dried fruit slices (see page 206)
2 teaspoons raw honey

Sweet treats, snacks and drinks

Snacking between meals isn't recommended in Ayurveda and in particular for Kapha types, as they can have a sluggish metabolism that needs a break. If you must eat something, I suggest a piece of poached fruit suitable for your dosha. The sweet flavour increases mucus in the body, so overall savoury snacks are better than sweet. Warm drinks are good for you, feel free to sip on these throughout your day.

Baby fig cakes

This is a revamped version of my mum's date loaf. When I first moved to Bangalow many moons ago I entered it in the Bangalow Show and won first prize. I was so damn proud. There is something about the tradition of handing down family recipes that I urge you all to hold on to tightly. It pains me that we have become so health obsessed we are letting recipes like this die because they are not deemed 'pure' enough. To use my mum's words, I think 'that's a load of codswallop' and the older I get the more I yearn for simplicity rather than the puritanical. There is nothing like sharing a homemade date loaf and I will choose a slice or two of my mum's over bliss balls every single time.

In this modified version I use less sugar and I've changed the flour, but it can be made with plain flour if that's all you have in the cupboard.

Preheat the oven to 180°C. Grease and line the base and sides of a 6 x ½ cup muffin holes or 23 cm x 13 cm loaf tin with baking paper.

Place the figs and ghee or butter in a saucepan, add 1 cup of water and bring to the boil. Reduce the heat and simmer for 10 minutes, until the figs are really soft. (This step is included because my mum uses packet dates from the supermarket and not those very expensive medjool dates.)

Remove the pan from the heat, add the bicarbonate of soda and mix to combine. Set aside and allow to cool.

Sift the flour, baking powder and spices into a bowl and stir in the sugar. Fold in the cooled fig mixture and the egg and milk, and gently mix until combined.

Spoon the mixture into the prepared muffin holes and press a fig into the centre, or spoon the mixture into a tin and place the figs down the middle. Bake the baby cakes for 15-20 minutes or the loaf for 40 minutes, until a skewer comes out clean when inserted in the centre. Allow to cool in the tin or muffin holes.

Makes 1 loaf or 6 baby cakes

1 cup (160 g) chopped dried juicy figs plus 6 juicy figs for on top

3 tablespoons ghee or butter

1 teaspoon bicarbonate of soda

1½ cups (180 g) gluten-free flour (I use a combo of buckwheat and brown rice)

1 teaspoon baking powder

1 teaspoon ground cinnamon

1 teaspoon ground cardamom

¼ teaspoon ground nutmeg

3 tablespoons coconut sugar

1 egg, lightly beaten

1 cup (250 ml) unhomogenised milk

Cacao, quinoa and orange fig balls

Place the figs, cacao powder and nibs, the spices, vanilla, orange zest and juice and quinoa in a food processor and process until the mixture forms a ball that comes away from the side of the bowl.

Roll teaspoons of the mixture into balls, then store in an airtight container for up to 1 week.

Makes 20 balls

8 soft dried figs, chopped
3 tablespoons cacao powder
2 tablespoons cacao nibs
1 teaspoon ground cinnamon
½ teaspoon ground cardamom
½ teaspoon vanilla powder
1 teaspoon orange zest
2 teaspoons orange juice
3 tablespoons puffed quinoa

Nori popcorn

Heat the ghee in a large saucepan, add the popping corn, cover with a lid and cook, shaking the pan once the corn starts popping to ensure all the corn kernels pop, over medium heat for 5 minutes, until the popping stops.

Remove the lid from the pan, add the salt, furikake and nutritional yeast and toss to coat the popcorn. Tip into a bowl and serve.

Serves 4

1 tablespoon ghee
1 cup (200 g) popping corn
pinch of sea salt
1 teaspoon furikake seasoning
1 teaspoon nutritional yeast

Jamu

This Balinese herbal tonic is antifungal, great for cleansing the blood and also works as an expectorant. The galangal is warming, so Pittas are better to use ginger. Jamu is particularly good for Kaphas who may have a lot of mucus or those with chesty colds.

Place the turmeric, galangal or ginger in a blender with 3 cups of water and blend until smooth.

Transfer to a saucepan, add the tamarind puree and sugar and bring to the boil. Reduce the heat and simmer for 20 minutes. Strain and cool. Store in a glass bottle in the refrigerator for up to 5 days.

Makes 3 cups

2 teaspoons grated fresh turmeric
1 teaspoon grated galangal or ginger
1 tablespoon tamarind puree
1 tablespoon grated palm sugar or coconut sugar

Dried fruit slices

Dried fruit is a good option for Kaphas. If you are going to make it regularly, I'd recommend investing in a mandoline so you can cut paper-thin slices of fruit. Then they will cook and dry out faster.

1 firm pear, very thinly sliced crossways on a mandoline

2 apples, very thinly sliced crossways on a mandoline

125 g fresh strawberries, halved

2 firm persimmons, very thinly sliced crossways on a mandoline

Preheat the oven to 150°C. Line two baking trays with baking paper.

Arrange the fruit on the lined trays and bake for 1-2 hours until dried. Turn off the oven and allow to cool in the oven. Store in an airtight container for up to 1 month.

Makes 2 cups

Metabolism booster morning shot

This is the perfect drink for Kaphas who are feeling heavy, sluggish or just blah. The cayenne pepper will give your metabolism a good kick and I recommend this to clients in winter if they can't move mucus from their sinus or chest.

a small pinch of cayenne pepper

½ lemon

Place the cayenne, lemon and 1 cup of water in a cup and mix to combine. Drink this after you have scraped your tongue and brushed your teeth to kickstart your digestive system.

Serves 1

Baba ganoush

Cook the whole eggplant on a barbecue or grill pan until very soft and the skin is charred. Set aside to cool.

Peel the eggplant and discard the skins. Place the eggplant flesh into a food processor, add garlic, lemon juice, tahini and cumin and process until smooth.

With the processor running, add the extra-virgin olive oil and puree until thick and creamy.

1 large eggplant

2 cloves garlic

1-2 tablespoons lemon juice

1 tablespoon tahini

1 teaspoon cumin

2 tablespoons extra-virgin olive oil

Beetroot yoghurt and sumac dip

Preheat oven to 180°C. Wrap the beetroot in foil and bake for 40 minutes or until very soft. Allow to cool, then peel. Grate the flesh into a bowl.

Add the garlic, yoghurt, chilli and sumac and mix to combine. Season with salt and allow to stand for 1 hour for the flavours to develop. Serve with vegetable sticks or buckwheat loaf.

Serves 4

1 beetroot

2 cloves garlic

½ cup (125 ml) yoghurt

dried chilli

sumac and ras el hanout to sprinkle

Hummus with smoky carrots

Place the carrots onto a barbecue or grill pan and cook until they are soft and slightly charred. Place the chickpeas, tahini, lemon juice, smoked salt, garlic and nutritional yeast into a food processor and process until smooth. With the processor running, add ½ cup (125 ml) water until the hummus is very creamy. Serve with charred carrots.

Serves 4

1 bunch baby carrots

1 can chickpeas

1 tablespoon hulled tahini

1 tablespoon lemon juice

a pinch of smoked salt

1 clove garlic

1-2 tablespoons nutritional yeast

Broccoli corn bread

Preheat the oven to 180°C. Grease and line the base and sides of
4 small loaf tins or a 20 x 10 cm loaf tin with baking paper.

Put the corn and 2 cups of water in a blender and blend until almost
smooth. Transfer to a bowl, add the broccoli, salt, nutritional yeast,
oil and polenta and mix well. Pour into the prepared tin and top
with the sliced onion and broccolini tips. Bake for 20–25 minutes for
the small loaves or 50 minutes for the large loaf tin, until a skewer
inserted in the centre comes out clean. Stand in the tin for 10 minutes,
then turn out onto a wire rack. Thickly slice and serve warm or cold.
Warm slices in the toaster or in a preheated oven.

2 cups (200 g) frozen corn kernels, thawed

2 cups (200 g) grated broccoli stalks and florets

1 teaspoon sea salt

1 teaspoon nutritional yeast

2 tablespoons extra-virgin olive oil

1 cup (190 g) fine polenta

1 small red onion, very thinly sliced

4 sprigs broccolini

Serves 8

Apple, celery, strawberry and ginger juice

You can keep the pulp from the juice and layer it with some coconut yoghurt and your choice of seeds for
a delicious snack.

Push the apple, celery, strawberry and ginger through a juicer. Stir
and serve.

6 green apples, cored and quartered

3 tender celery stalks

8 fresh strawberries, hulled

a thumb-sized piece of ginger

Serves 4

Food medicine

These recipes are for when your tummy really isn't very happy or you're feeling stressed and ungrounded or generally a little off-colour.

It is important that Vata types don't skip meals, even when they are feeling poorly; just make your meals small or sup on soup or broth. Vatas: if your tummy is fragile, I recommend you make ghee your best friend and pop it in your porridge, warm drinks and meals. Try to avoid chilled raw foods, especially in winter when your digestive system can be vulnerable to the dry cold weather.

Heat is usually the issue when Pittas are sick. You want to aim to keep your temperature down. Opt for chicken stock rather than beef stock (which is heating), but if you are feeling weak or have been sick for some time, you may need beef bone broth to improve your strength.

When Kaphas are off colour, food may be the last thing you feel like and it is okay for you to miss a meal here or there. Opt to drop breakfast and dinner rather than lunch. Avoid any foods that create mucus when you are unwell as, in most cases, this will aggravate your condition further. You will do well to sip on herbal teas that will warm and dry up any moisture in your body.

For all doshas

Ghee

Ghee is simply clarified butter. I am often asked why I am so obsessed with ghee. The reason is if there was to be one superfood in Ayurveda, it would be ghee. It is suitable for all doshas (Kaphas need a little less than other doshas) and can be used both internally and externally. It is a rich source of butyric acid, which helps feed and grow healthy gut bacteria. Ghee increases agni (digestive fire), controls bad gut bacteria, regulates irregular bowel movements and calms appetite by giving you an increased feeling of satiety. It is considered the king of Ayurvedic food medicine, especially for Vata types. Air travel can cause imbalance for Vatas, so add ghee to your drinks and meals while you are away.

To make your own ghee, all you need to do is heat the butter to separate the milk solids. In India, the milk solids are mixed with sugar and enjoyed as a sweet. Ghee should be kept at room temperature, not in the fridge, and stored out of direct sunlight. It has a very high smoke point, so is an extremely versatile cooking medium.

250 g organic butter

Place the butter in a small heavy-based saucepan over medium heat and cook, without stirring, for 10–15 minutes. At first the butter will bubble and sometimes spit, then a bubbling white foam will form on top, and finally the foam will become very still. If you tilt the pan, you will see the milk solids on the base have turned golden brown, imparting a lovely nutty flavour to the clarified butter. Be careful at this point because the milk solids can easily catch and burn, tainting the flavour.

Remove the pan from the heat. Line a metal sieve with paper towel, a clean Chux or some muslin and place over a glass jug or bowl. Strain the golden liquid into the jug or bowl, leaving the brown milk solids in the bottom of the pan.

Store the ghee in a clean glass jar at room temperature. It will solidify as it cools.

Makes 1 cup

Milk for sleep

Place the milk in a saucepan, add the ghee, nutmeg, saffron, cinnamon and cardamom and cook over low–medium heat without boiling for 10 minutes.

Serve sweetened with your choice of sweetener: Kapha and Vata can use honey (it is too heating for Pitta), Pitta can use maple syrup or coconut sugar.

Serves 2

2 cups (500 ml) unhomogenised cow's milk

1 teaspoon ghee

¼ teaspoon freshly grated nutmeg

pinch saffron

1 teaspoon ground cinnamon

1 teaspoon ground cardamom

raw honey, pure maple syrup or coconut sugar, to sweeten

Digestive tea

This tea stimulates digestion and calms Pitta. Vata and Pitta may want to sweeten this drink, Kapha types should avoid doing so.

Pour 2 cups of boiling water into a small teapot, add the spices, rose petals and coriander leaves and allow to stand for 5 minutes. Strain into cups and drink.

Serves 2

¼ teaspoon cumin seeds

¼ teaspoon coriander seeds

¼ teaspoon fennel seeds

¼ teaspoon dried rose petals

¼ teaspoon coriander leaves

Warming Vata kitchari

Kitchari, as you may have gathered by now, is the go-to Ayurvedic food medicine. It will soothe and help heal a fragile Vata tummy and is the foundation of most cleanses in Ayurveda. If you are a Vata experiencing gut issues, I recommend you find yourself a place that sells split mung dhal and stock up on them so you always have some on hand to make kitchari.

Kitchari is such a powerful food medicine because it is incredibly soothing for the digestive system. The following recipe makes enough for four people but I suggest halving the grains if you are on your own as Ayurveda isn't a fan of leftovers, especially when we are using food as a medicine. Freshly cooked is always considered far more healing and therapeutic than frozen or precooked foods.

Soak the basmati rice and mung dhal in cold water for 2 hours. Rinse and drain.

Melt the ghee in a large, deep frying pan, add the spices and cook over medium heat for 1 minute, until the seeds start to dance in the pan.

Add the onion, garlic and ginger to the pan and cook, stirring occasionally, for 10 minutes, until the onion is soft and golden. Stir in the vegetables and cook for 5 minutes, until they start to soften. Stir in the rice and mung dhal, saffron and 1.25 litres of water and a generous pinch of salt, and bring to the boil. Cook over high heat until tunnels appear in the surface of the rice, about 10 minutes. Reduce the heat and simmer for 15 minutes, until the rice and mung dhal are soft and slightly mushy.

Turn off the heat. Squeeze over the lemon juice and season with salt.

Serves 4

½ cup (200 g) basmati rice

¼ cup (150 g) split mung dhal

3 tablespoons ghee

1 teaspoon each of cumin seeds, coriander seeds, black mustard seeds, ground turmeric

1 cinnamon stick

4 cloves

4 cardamom pods, bruised

1 onion, finely chopped

2 garlic cloves, grated

1 tablespoon grated ginger

3 cups (600 g) chopped or grated vegetables (such as carrots, beans, broccoli, zucchini)

sea salt

a generous pinch of saffron threads

juice of 1 lemon

Miso mushroom soup

Put the water into a large saucepan, add the spring onion, mushroom, ginger and wakame and bring to boil. Reduce heat and simmer for 15 minutes.

Blend the miso with 2 tablespoons of hot water and add to the pan, do not allow the stock to boil once you have done this.

Makes 1 litre

4 cups (1 L) water
2 spring onions, sliced
3 dried shiitake mushrooms, broken into pieces
50g enoki mushrooms, broken into small pieces
2cm piece of ginger, finely julienned
2 tablespoons broken dried wakame or kombu
2 tablespoons shiro miso

Kapha reducing tea

Place the spices and lemon juice into a cup, pour over the boiling water and stir to combine.

Allow to stand until warm and then sweeten with honey.

1 teaspoon grated ginger
1 teaspoon fenugreek seeds
2 teaspoons lemon juice
1 cup (250 ml) boiling water
1 teaspoon honey

Pepper milk

Place the pepper, milk and 3 tablespoons of water in a saucepan and bring to the boil, stirring constantly. Simmer until reduced to 1 cup. Pour into a cup and drink.

Serves 1

½ teaspoon freshly ground black pepper
1 cup (250 ml) unhomogenised cow's milk

Miso ramen broth

Place the chicken wings, onion, carrot, spring onion, ginger, garlic, mirin, tamari and 3 litres of water in a stockpot and bring to the boil. Reduce the heat to low and simmer, partially covered, for 2 hours. Strain the stock into a large saucepan.

Blend the miso with a little of the hot stock and stir into the stock in the pan. Return to the heat, add the sriracha (if using) and gently heat without boiling for 15 minutes.

Makes about 2 litres

1 kg chicken wings
1 onion, roughly chopped
2 carrots, chopped
8 spring onions, chopped
½ cup sliced ginger
1 garlic bulb, halved
2 tablespoons mirin
2 tablespoons tamari
3 tablespoons aka miso
1 tablespoon sriracha chilli sauce (optional)

Nourishing chicken soup with rice and spice and all things nice

I adore chicken soup and truly believe it is one of the best food medicines in the world. Daikon is really good medicine for the large intestine.

Place the chicken in a stockpot, add the onion, celery, carrot, daikon, rice, garlic, ginger and spices and pour in 3 litres of water. Bring to the boil, then reduce the heat to low and simmer, partially covered, for 2 hours. Remove the chicken, discard the skin and bones and return the flesh to the pan.

Add the parsnip, zucchini, cauliflower, salt and tamari and cook for 1 hour more. Season before serving.

Makes 2.5 litres

1 x 1.6 kg chicken

1 onion, chopped

3 celery stalks, chopped

2 carrots, roughly chopped

2 daikon, sliced

½ cup (100 g) basmati rice, optional

1 garlic bulb, halved

a thumb-sized piece of ginger, sliced

1 cinnamon stick

3 star anise

3 cloves

6 black peppercorns

1 bay leaf

2 parsnips, peeled and sliced

2 zucchini, sliced

250 g cauliflower, cut into small florets

a generous pinch of sea salt

1 tablespoon tamari

Chicken stock

I always keep the carcass and bones from my roast chicken to make stock.

Place the chicken frames and wings in a stockpot, add the vegetables, bay leaf, peppercorns and 4–6 litres of water. (Alternatively, place the ingredients in a slow cooker.) Bring to the boil, reduce the heat to a gentle simmer and cook, partially covered, for 8 hours or overnight.

Strain the stock into a jug or bowl and discard the bones and vegetables. Allow the stock to cool, then cover and refrigerate overnight. The next day, remove the fat that has set on top and transfer to another container to reserve for cooking or discard. Use the stock immediately or pour into containers (leaving a little room for it to expand if you are freezing it), seal and store in the refrigerator for up to 4 days or freeze for up to 3 months.

Makes about 3 litres

2 chicken frames

1 kg chicken wings

1 onion, roughly chopped

2 carrots, roughly chopped

3 celery stalks, roughly chopped

1 bay leaf

6 black peppercorns

Gentle on the tummy congee

The first yoga I studied had its origin in macrobiotics so my spring cleanse regime always consisted of congee. I still find it to be wonderfully cleansing and one of the most soothing food medicines for my body. For years I ate brown rice congee but these days I lean more towards white rice congee and use basmati rice, as it is the best for Vata types. Please make your own stock for this or buy a really good-quality organic one.

I like to cook my congee in a slow cooker as it saves me having to worry about it catching on the bottom of the pan. You can vary the toppings, but when I am having it as a healing food, I keep it pretty simple.

Place the rice, stock, kombu, sliced ginger, ghee and sesame oil in a saucepan, cover and cook over medium heat for 1–1½ hours, stirring several times to prevent the rice from catching on the bottom of the pan. (Alternatively, cook for 4 hours in a slow cooker on the highest setting.)

Serve the congee in bowls, topped with the furikake, gomasio or sesame seeds, spring onion, pickled ginger and coriander leaves and finished with some white pepper (if using) and a dob of ghee.

Serves 4

½ cup (100 g) basmati rice

1.5 litres homemade Vegetable or Chicken Stock (pages 220 and 224)

a piece of kombu

3 thin slices of ginger

1 tablespoon ghee, plus extra to serve

1 tablespoon toasted sesame oil

3 tablespoons furikake or gomasio or toasted sesame seeds

3 spring onions, sliced

2 tablespoons pickled ginger, finely shredded

a handful of coriander leaves

freshly ground white pepper, to serve (optional)

The secret to living well and longer is: eat half, walk double, laugh triple and love without measure

—Tibetan proverb

The stock story

There is nothing like homemade stock. I like to sip on it as a medicine when I am sick or have no appetite as it is effective food medicine, but I don't recommend you live on it for long periods.

Beef stock

The browner you roast your bones, the richer your stock will be, and the longer you simmer it, the better it will taste.

Preheat the oven to 180°C.

Place the marrow bones and onion in a roasting tin and roast for 1 hour until browned.

Transfer the bones and onion to a stockpot, add the vegetables, bay leaf, peppercorns and 4–6 litres of water. (Alternatively, you can use a slow cooker.) Bring to the boil, reduce the heat to a gentle simmer and cook, partially covered, for 8 hours or overnight.

Strain the stock into a jug or bowl and discard the bones and vegetables. Allow the stock to cool, then cover and refrigerate overnight. The next day, remove the fat that has set on top and transfer to another container to reserve for cooking or discard. Use immediately or pour the stock into containers (leaving a little room for it to expand if you are freezing it), seal and store in the refrigerator for up to 4 days or freeze for up to 3 months.

Makes about 3 litres

1 kg beef marrow bones
1 onion, roughly chopped
2 carrots, roughly chopped
3 celery stalks, roughly chopped
1 bay leaf
6 black peppercorns

Vegetable bouillon paste

I give my vegetable stock an extra boost of flavour with herbs and spices. In winter I like to add ginger, turmeric and chopped coriander; if I want more of an Asian vibe I'll stir in cinnamon, cloves and star anise. If I'm using the stock in Italian-style dishes, I'll include dried oregano and chopped parsley. Play around and see what works for you. A rule to remember: do not use starchy vegetables as they will make your stock cloudy.

Place the vegetables, nutritional yeast and salt into a food processor and process until you have a rough paste. Allow to sit for 30 minutes or until the salt draws the moisture out of the vegetables. Drain well. Freeze the vegetable bouillon paste in ice cube trays and use a couple in 1 litre of water to make a delicious vegetable stock.

Makes 2 cups

1 onion, roughly chopped
1 leek, white part only, sliced (optional)
2 carrots, chopped
3 celery stalks, chopped
200g broccoli stalk and florets
2 tablespoons nutritional yeast
1 tablespoon salt

Herbal teas and medicated milks

Vata

Vata types should avoid bitter, astringent or cooling teas and instead favour more warming options.

Recommended teas: Anise, basil, bay, cardamom, celery seeds, cinnamon, cloves, eucalyptus, fennel, fenugreek, ginger, licorice, nutmeg, orange peel.

Pitta

Heating teas should be avoided by Pitta types.

Recommended teas: Alfalfa, blackberry, chamomile, chicory, chrysanthemum, comfrey, coriander, cumin, dandelion, fennel, hibiscus, jasmine, lemon, lemon balm, lemongrass, licorice, lime, nettle, peppermint, rose, saffron, spearmint.

Kapha

Most herbal teas are suitable except those containing licorice, as it is sweet and mucus forming.

Recommended teas: Alfalfa, basil, blackberry, black pepper, cardamom, celery seeds, chamomile, cinnamon, cloves, dandelion, dill, eucalyptus, ginger, hawthorn, juniper berries, lemon, mustard seeds, nettle, orange peel, parsley, peppermint, sage, spearmint, thyme.

Masala chai for all Doshas

This warming chai is suitable for all doshas in the cold but Pitta types need to lower the ginger in summer.

To make the masala chai blend, place the spices in a bowl and mix to combine.

Place 2 teaspoons of masala chai blend in each cup, top up with boiling water and warm milk. Finish with your choice of sweetener and stir well. Alternatively, for a more concentrated chai, simmer 1 to 2 tablespoons masala chai blend in 1.25 litres of water with 3 rooibos teabags for 15 minutes, then add the milk to the pan and cook for 5 minutes more.

1 tablespoon ground ginger

1 tablespoon ground cinnamon

2 teaspoons ground cardamom

2 teaspoons ground fennel

1 teaspoon ground cloves

¼ teaspoon freshly ground black pepper

½ cup (125 ml) warm frothy milk

honey or maple syrup

Serves 4

NOTE:

Vata – coconut milk, almond milk, cow's milk. Vata types can have more milk as it is warming for their dosha.

Pitta – coconut milk, cow's milk, rice milk. Pittas need to take care with oilier types of milk as they can be overheating for them; examples are almond milk and soy milk.

Kapha – soy milk, rice milk, coconut milk. Kaphas need just a splash of milk, too much will aggravate their dosha.

The Ayurvedic pantry

Nuts and seeds

All nuts and seeds are sweet, warming and heavy which is why nuts in particular need to be eaten only in small amounts by Pitta and Kapha types. The fattier the nuts – macadamia, cashews, walnuts, pistachios and pine nuts – the less suited they are to these doshas. Salted roasted nuts are even more heating and are best avoided by Pittas, especially in summer.

Almonds are highly regarded in Ayurveda. They are considered rejuvenative but need to be prepared properly and it is not recommended they form the base of every meal no matter what dosha you are. Almonds must be soaked in cold water and then peeled as their skins make them difficult to digest. Vata types can eat almonds freely but Pitta and Kapha need to exercise restraint, like with all other nuts, as they are heating and high in fat, and this aggravates these doshas.

Vata – Nuts will ground Vata but they take a bit to digest so avoid making a meal out of them if you have issues with your digestion.

Pitta – Vegetarian Pitta and Kapha doshas who still need to use nuts and seeds as a protein source should still do this but I suggest cooling digestive spices or coconut be added to nut meals to remedy the issues we have discussed. Coconuts, however, are cooling and are perfect medicine for fiery Pittas.

Kapha – Nuts form mucus in the body so Kapha types who struggle with excess mucus need to break up with them.

Dairy

The cow is sacred in India and its fresh milk is considered very therapeutic for Vata and Pitta. However, western milk production is a far cry from having a cow out the back and with the advent of pasteurisation and homogenisation, milk is a very different liquid now than it was 5000 years ago. Ayurveda recommends that all milk be consumed warm as it makes it more digestible, and adding spices will further enhance its absorption. With all dairy, I recommend consuming organic dairy products.

Vata – Good quality dairy is cooling, heavy and nourishing but difficult for Vata types to assimilate. If you are a Vata type and want to drink milk, please ensure you warm it first and add some warming spices to it such as cinnamon and cardamom. Fermented dairy is heating so Vatas can enjoy yoghurt, buttermilk and sour cream. Chilled smoothies and frozen yoghurt ice-cream will aggravate Vata, especially when consumed on cold or windy days.

Pitta – Fiery Pittas enjoy the cooling they gain from dairy but they need to be careful with heating aged or brined cheeses such as parmesan or feta. Yoghurt and other fermented dairy can also increase their fire and should be consumed in moderation. Coconut yoghurt is a good option. Pittas can enjoy ice-cream in summer as their robust digestive system is better equipped to deal with its chilling properties.

Kapha – Most Kaphas love dairy but unfortunately it doesn't love them and they do best to steer clear of it. Dairy can lead to excess mucus production and this is something Kaphas already struggle with. Young children who are in the Kapha phase of their life can get very mucousy and limiting how much milk and yoghurt they consume will often provide relief for those kids who are plagued with constant snotty noses. If Kapha children insist on having milk, warming it and making sure it is unhomogenised will make it a little easier to digest.

Oils

In Ayurveda, ghee is our most valued cooking medium because it is considered to be light and very easy to digest for all the doshas. For salad dressings, organic sunflower oil is an oil that is suitable for the three doshas.

Olive oil is warming and heavy so it is best suited to Vata types but may aggravate Pitta if used in excess, especially in summer and even more so when heated. It can also disturb Kapha because of its heavy nature.

Sesame oil is hot and heavy and is the perfect oil for grounding Vata; however, it is often too heating for Pitta in the warmer months and too heavy for Kapha. Toasted sesame oil is even more warming and dense so should be used in moderation by Kapha and Pitta.

Coconut oil, unsalted butter and avocado oils are cooling so these are a good choice for Pitta but are not recommended for Kapha and Vata.

In general, nut, seed and bean oils, oily vegetable oils and animal fats are all warming, sweet and heavy. They would all benefit Vata because it is cool, light and dry in nature.

Kapha types need to maintain awareness around oil consumption (including ghee) as excess oil in the diet can lead to weight gain and this is often an issue for folks of this dosha.

Be calmly active and actively calm.
That is the way of the yogi.
–Paramahansa Yogananda

Animal foods

Vata – Of all the doshas who can tolerate red meat, Vata is the most capable. Meat is heavy and heating and will calm Vata; however, they don't need much to provide them with what they may be craving. Fish, chicken and eggs are all great protein sources for Vata and eggs are particularly calming for Vata. A warm egg based breakfast makes a great start to the day for Vata types.

Pitta – Red meat is heating and Pitta do best to limit their consumption, especially in summer. Chicken and fresh water fish are cooling enough for Pitta types to eat. Seafood, with the exception of prawns, is heating and can aggravate Pitta easily, some may even be allergic to it. Egg yolks are also heating so egg consumption should be moderated in the hotter months; however, egg white is cooling so they can be separated and used instead.

Kapha – Red meat is difficult to digest and because of Kaphas' sluggish digestive system they should limit their consumption, especially in the cooler months. Chicken is OK for them but they don't need much and white meat is better for them than the dark meat. Eggs should be consumed in moderation.

Fruit

Fruit is considered a pure food in Ayurveda that is satisfying and calming. It is good for relieving thirst and settling the stomach. Eat fruit that is in season and grown locally. There are a number of fruits that can be enjoyed by all three doshas, mango is the main one, along with purple grapes, cherries, apricots and berries. Bananas are heavy and moist and great for Vata, but can create mucus in the body so Kaphas should warm them with spices and avoid them in winter. Cooked apples and pears are suitable for all doshas. However, uncooked apples and pears can aggravate Vata. Dried fruit is good for Kapha and Pitta but will aggravate Vata. Raisins that have been soaked overnight are suitable for all doshas and are used as a digestive remedy.

Vata – Most fruit is cooling and light so it is suitable for Vata types when they are balanced. Crisp dry fruits like apples and pears can be very aggravating for Vata types, but cooking them with ghee and spices reduces these qualities so best to eat them cooked instead.

Pitta – Pittas can enjoy ripe sweet fruits and will really appreciate them in summer when they are struggling with the heat, probably why we crave those delicious tropical fruits when we are holidaying in Asia. Sour fruits are heating and are best enjoyed in the cooler months when they are in season.

Kapha – Kaphas can enjoy fruit but not in the quantities the other doshas are free to, as the sweet quality of fruit increases water in the body and may lead to a build up of mucus. This is why it is good to limit fruit in winter or when you have a chesty cold. Grapefruit, pomegranate and lemon are good for reducing mucus. Sweet fruit lowers agni (digestive fires) and Kaphas can't really afford to have the digestive flame lowered. Bananas are heavy and mucus forming and should be avoided by Kaphas and children in winter and spring.

Vegetables

Not all vegetables are suitable for all doshas.

Avocados are moist and cooling and best suited to Pittas, Vatas can eat them in the hotter months and Kaphas do best without them.

Beetroot is sweet and warming, making it the perfect vegetable choice for Vata and Kapha when eaten raw. Pittas can tolerate beetroot if it is cooked.

Brassicas, which include brussels sprouts, cabbages, kale, cauliflower and broccoli, are drying and cooling and are good medicine for Pitta and Kapha but they can affect the thyroid. Kapha types with thyroid issues need to be mindful of the effect on their body. Vata types need to limit consumption of brassicas as they are gas forming and can irritate their sensitive guts.

Capsicums (bell peppers) are sweet, astringent and cooling, making them suitable for Pitta and Kapha but they need to be eaten in moderation by Vata, especially in the cooler months.

Carrots are heating when raw so they are good for Kapha but aggravate Vata and Pitta if they eat too many. Cooked carrots are a lot more favourable for all three doshas but because they become sweet when cooked they are particularly beneficial for Vata and Pitta. Carrots can have a cleansing effect on the body so are great to include in juices, especially for Kapha.

Corn is heating and drying so in excess it will aggravate both Pitta and Vata but is suitable for Kapha.

Eggplant is generally cooling and best eaten in summer. It may aggravate Pitta if eaten in excess because of its high water content. Eggplant is best prepared with pungent warming vegetables and spices such as onion, garlic and pepper.

Mushrooms are sweet, astringent and pungent. They take moisture out of the body so they are a great food for Kapha types who can have issues with fluid retention. Mushrooms are not recommended for Vata types because of their drying nature.

Potatoes, pumpkin and **sweet potato** are heavy, sweet and cooling and recommended for Vata and Pitta but can create mucus in Kapha.

Pungent vegetables, which include onion, leek, garlic, radish and chilli, are stimulating. Onions when raw will aggravate all three doshas and it is very rare to see raw onion in Ayurvedic recipes. Fiery Pitta types should avoid consuming them raw. Cooking mellows pungent vegetables a little and makes them suitable for Kapha and Vata but some Pittas find they still suffer heartburn if they consume them when they are out of balance. Garlic is heating and it aggravates Pitta, especially when raw because of its warming properties. It is said to prevent gas so it is recommended for calming Vata.

Tomatoes are a member of the nightshade family. They are sour, heating and sweet. In excess they will aggravate all three doshas when eaten raw and you will find a lot of people have a natural aversion to uncooked tomato. Cooking tomatoes with cumin, turmeric and mustard seeds warms them and makes them more digestible.

Vata – Vata types need to cook their vegetables with plenty of oil, and eat them warm to remedy the light quality that vegetables that grow up and out of the ground have. Serving greens with oil dressing or tahini is a good way to make them more digestible. Raw vegetables are not recommended for Vata types in the cooler, windier months; if you do have a craving for salad at this time of year, ensure it is dressed with warming oil and vinegar.

Pitta – Pittas are fortunate that they can enjoy most vegetables. The only ones that may present a problem for them are the nightshades – tomatoes, eggplant, capsicum and potatoes. These are heating and acid forming and aggravate the fire in Pittas, especially in summer. Silverbeet and spinach are also heating in nature so Pittas are better to choose kale, bok choy or lettuce for their greens. Raw vegetables will cool Pittas but should really only be eaten in summer when their digestive fire is in its prime.

Kapha – Kaphas need to make friends with vegetables. Most vegetables are dry and light and perfect for the heavy qualities of the water and earth in the Kapha dosha. Kaphas should cook their vegetables but prepare them with a minimal amount of oil. Carrot and celery are good vegetables for Kapha types as they help to reduce excess water in the body, an issue that Kaphas can struggle with, especially when they travel.

Adding warming spices to cooked vegetables will warm them. Avoid using too much salt with vegetables as salt increases moisture in the body.

Grains

Vata – Vata can enjoy most grains, as they are heavy, grounding and nourishing. Introducing grains to your diet is recommended if you have a fragile tummy, especially basmati rice as it is considered very easy to digest. The only grains that will aggravate Vata are the more light drying grains such as rye, millet, polenta, barley and corn. Breads often aggravate Vata but this is because the grains are mixed with yeast and sugar, which then make them heavier and causes gas and bloating. Dried grains, which as the name indicates are dry in nature, will aggravate Vata so that is why porridge is better for Vata types than muesli. Crackers, crisp breads and corn chips will also disturb Vata too and I often find they love them and resist giving up their chip and dip obsession.

Pitta – Grains are good for Pittas, as they are calming and balancing without being too heating. Of all the doshas, Pitta is most able to eat a wide variety of grains, and will tend to be able to tolerate wheat where the other doshas will struggle with its cooling nature.

Kapha – Kapha types struggle with grains. The heavy grounding nature increases the Kapha qualities. Rye, millet, polenta, barley and buckwheat are all fantastic grain choices for Kapha, as they are all warming, light and drying.

Beans and pulses

Beans can be difficult to digest and all doshas should take care not to overdo them in their diet. Lentils and mung beans are easier to digest than beans, and split mung beans are the most gut-friendly for all the doshas of all the bean and pulse family. Split mung beans are light and gently cooling and are considered extremely therapeutic in Ayurvedic cooking and the easiest to digest for all doshas. As with all cooling foods, Vata and Kapha do well to warm them up with warming spices – black pepper, ginger, clove, five spice, nutmeg, cinnamon, cumin and mustard seeds. Whole mung beans are not as digestible as their split sisters. Rinsing sprouting beans everyday for 3 days will increase their digestibility.

Vata – Vata and beans don't really see eye to eye. The cooling and drying nature of beans aggravate Vatas and they are best to stick to split mung beans and tofu. If you insist on having beans, cooking them with some asafoetida (hing) or digestive spices (coriander, cumin, fennel, ginger) will help but please don't overdo the consumption of them or it will be: Beans 1 Vata 0.

Pitta – Red kidneys are specific Pitta food medicine, but all other doshas do best to stay away from these guys as they are cooling and will increase Vata and Kapha. Pittas can deal with beans a little better than the other doshas but it is still recommended that they team them with the digestive spices or at least some cumin.

Kapha – Beans are light and drying so perfect for Kapha types but you still need to be aware of their tendencies to create gas in the body. Soaking beans overnight is essential and cooking them until soft will help to alleviate some of the gas issues. Cooking them with digestives spices such as cumin, coriander and fennel will also help. Tofu, which is a soy bean derivative, can be enjoyed on rare occasions for Kapha as it is a bit too heavy and cooling. Vegetarians and vegans are better opting for tempeh, which is fermented and more warming.

Sweet stuff

Vata – Vata will benefit from the grounding nature of sweeteners. The sweet taste is good for calming Vata but this does not give you license to inhale lollies and cakes. Raw desserts can be aggravating for Vata when they are made with too much cooling coconut oil. Vata will do best getting a sweet fix from eating sweet fruit cooked in the cooler months, and complex carbohydrate sweet vegetables such as pumpkin and sweet potato. Honey is more warming than maple syrup and is your best sweetener to use in drinks.

Pitta – The sweet flavour will cool and calm Pitta and might be what they find themselves craving when they are angry or stressed. Pitta can eat fresh raw honey, which is cooling, or maple syrup is also an option for them.

Kapha – The sweet flavour will quickly unbalance Kapha so they do best avoiding it, as it creates moisture in the body and leads to weight gain. Honey can be used to absorb moisture in the body in combination with lemon and cayenne.

Chocolate

Chocolate is moist, heavy and heating and tolerated best by Vata types. The caffeine in it will stimulate Pitta so if they do choose to eat it, do it before 4pm. Kaphas love chocolate but unless it is bitter dark chocolate they are reaching for, they will find their mucous Kapha tendencies quickly increased due to its sweet moist nature.

Honey

Raw honey is a wonderful food and medicine, suitable in moderation for both Vata and Kapha but considered a bit too heating for Pitta types; however, some schools of thought say fresh from the hive honey is OK for Pitta types. As honey ages, it becomes more warming. Ayurveda is really funny about heating honey and we would never boil it, even when it is added to hot drinks we advise that the drink shouldn't be piping hot. Buy good honey, local if possible as they say that honey sourced from local regions can remedy asthma.

What you seek
is seeking you.
–Rumi

The Ayurvedic spice cupboard

Spices are used as medicine in the Ayurvedic kitchen, and they can be used to increase the digestive properties of a meal or as a way of removing impurities from the body.

My spice cupboard is used more than my pantry. I buy organic spices when I can and I make sure I buy them from a place where I know they are fresh because you can really taste the difference, especially with turmeric. Stale turmeric tastes like dirt and fresh turmeric is sweet and wonderfully aromatic.

You don't need a ridiculously large amount of spices; in fact, if you start with the basics, you can just keep topping these up and buy others when you need them.

I suggest always having supplies of cinnamon, coriander (seed and ground), cumin (seed and ground), fennel seed, cardamom, turmeric, ginger, clove, fenugreek, mustard seeds (I like black and they look pretty), star anise, bay leaf and garam masala.

Spices are best stored in glass jars with a tight seal, and roasting them dry or in ghee will add to the flavour of a meal.

Grinding spices awakens energies in the body. Grind it, inhale it. The smell wakes you up and awakens ancestral memories.

Asafoetida (hing)
Calms Vata, aids assimilation, potent calmative. Given to breastfeeding mothers to increase milk production. A strong medicine; use sparingly for Vata and Kapha.

Black pepper
Increases Pitta, decreases Vata and Kapha. Aggravates Pitta in excess – very drying to the body. Stimulates digestion and heats the body, best suited to Kapha and Vata types because of its warming properties. Pitta types need to reduce consumption in summer or if they are feeling overheated.

Cardamom
Cardamom is believed to open the heart, calm the mind, provide an uplifting feeling to one's spirit. Cardamom is known as the Queen of Spices and helps us to be present in the here and now.

Ayurveda loves cardamom for its digestion stimulating qualities and its ability to balance ALL three doshas. Cardamom is used to calm Vata, especially in kids with funny tummies. Teamed with fennel it balances agni and can relieve vomiting, burping and reflux. Cardamom has been used for many years by traditional cultures as a breath freshener and in the treatment of mouth ulcers. It is particularly good for Kaphas as it can be used to reduce phlegm from the nose and sinuses.

Cardamom is often combined with fennel to balance agni. Mix ½ teaspoon each cardamom and fennel in hot water and sip throughout the day to build digestive fire (agni).

In excess, cardamom aggravates Pitta. Mix with liquorice and fennel to reduce acidity.

Cayenne

Increases Vata and Pitta because it is drying. Great for Kapha as it pulls the excess moisture out of the cells, great for water retention, excess phlegm and mucus. Considered a strong and beneficial medicine in Ayurveda, because it stimulates the circulatory and digestive system.

* Caution. Monitor use if you have an inflammatory condition.*

Cinnamon

Warms and sweetens, aids digestion. Strong diaphoretic and expectorant, and recommended for those who are weak or unwell. It can help with toothaches as it has mild pain relieving properties. It is better for Pitta types to use as it won't increase heat in the body like ginger tends to. Cinnamon is said to increase heart energy and tonify the kidneys.

Coriander

Cooling, soothing, calmative and digestive. The leaves and seeds are used to calm Pitta aggravation in the digestive and urinary system because of their cooling qualities. Fresh coriander juice can be used to treat heat conditions in the skin. Coriander leaves can be used by all doshas.

Clove

Heating, aids digestion. Their warming qualities mean they can help with chills, colds and coughs and clove oil is often used with toothaches because of its analgesic properties.

* People with high blood pressure, inflammation or increased Pitta need to exercise caution when using cloves.*

Cumin

Calmative, digestive, balances all doshas. Helps to stimulate digestion and absorption and can be used to treat conditions of heat in the digestive system like diarrhoea. Cumin is often added to heating foods such as tomatoes and chillis to cool and make them more digestible.

Curry leaf (neem)

Cooling, bitter, clears and removes wastes. The main ingredient in curries in India. They cool Pitta and are also used for treatment in weight loss and diabetes.

Fennel seeds

Another one of Ayurveda's top digestives spices, it strengthens agni and increases the downward flow of energy, reduces bloating. Can aid digestion in young and elderly. Balances Vata, Pitta, Kapha – and is very good for Vata types as it helps to calm the nervous system. Great to roast and eat after meals – eat a teaspoonful. Aids digestive process and helps food to move through digestive system. Cools, sweetens, aids digestion, tonifying to the stomach. Fennel is also believed to be beneficial in promoting menstruation and aiding milk flow in breastfeeding mothers.

Fenugreek (methi)

Warming, aids digestion, tonifying, reduces mass. Good for the nervous, respiratory and reproductive systems. It is a bitter seed and works best in dhal, pickles and spice mixes. Fenugreek is very beneficial for Kapha types and can also be used by Vata.

Not to be used by pregnant women as can cause miscarriage or bleeding, can aggravate Pitta.

Flaxseed

Recommended for Vata to help heal the gut. Flaxseeds are said to help heal and tonify lung tissue. Because of this, they are recommended for Kaphas or anyone with respiratory issues. They can be combined with psyllium and used as a laxative for Vata or mixed with honey as an expectorant. Also flaxseed can be mixed with water to treat constipation.

Garlic

Warming, strengthening, reduces ama. Garlic is very therapeutic and has very strong detoxifying properties. It helps remove ama and move Kapha from the blood and lymph. Recommended as a bit of a cure-all for Vata types.

Ginger

Increases agni, brings Kapha down, warms Vata up. Heating, toning, cleansing.

Ayurveda recognises ginger as the most balancing and calming of all spices. It works wonders on the digestive and respiratory systems. Use it for nausea, travel sickness, gas and cramping, including menstrual cramps. Mixed with salt, it calms Vata; mixed with rock candy (sugar), it balances Pitta; mixed with honey, it relieves Kapha. Dry ginger is great for Kapha as it can move mucus from the lungs. Shots made with ginger, black pepper and cayenne are good for excess mucus. Fill a small shot glass with hot water, add 1 tablespoon ginger juice, a pinch of cayenne and some cracked black pepper and drink it in one go.

In excess, ginger will create imbalance in Pitta. Note dry ginger is hotter than fresh ginger so Pitta types be warned.

Hibiscus flowers

Sweet, cooling and astringent. Recommended for kidney, skin and reproductive issues.

* Avoid if you are in a state of high Vata or anxiety.

Licorice

Sweet, bitter, cooling. Great for Pitta, Vata in moderation and not great for Kapha.

* Not recommended for high Kapha imbalance – fluid retention, high blood pressure or osteoporosis – as it inhibits the absorption of calcium and potassium.

Mustard seeds

Very warming, aid digestion, especially black mustard seeds. Not recommended for Pitta in summer.

Nutmeg

Pungent and heating, used to treat insomnia. Grate the nutmeg fresh and use it in milk to bring on sleep. Ayurveda uses it along with cinnamon and cardamom in milk as a bedtime remedy. It is great for calming Vata. Nutmeg also can increase absorption in the small intestine and is often teamed with cardamom and ginger to do this.

Saffron

Cools, tonifies digestive system, balances all doshas.

Sesame seeds

Sweet and warming, sesame seeds are considered to be incredibly healing for Vata types. They are beneficial for the bones and the teeth, and the Japanese make a mix of sesame seeds and salt called gomasio. Use white or black. Black sesame oil is warmed and applied to the skin to calm Vata anxiety.

Turmeric

Turmeric is tridoshic, which means it balances all three doshas. It aids the digestion of meat and proteins and has some anti-inflammatory and anti-oxidant properties, as well as scraping cholesterol out of blood and impurities out of the digestive system. It is used to kindle agni and reduce toxins in the body. Traditionally in Ayurveda it is used to support the blood, liver, joints and immune system. Mix it with ginger for infections, coughs or colds. Add cayenne if there is mucus. Needs black pepper or coconut oil to aid absorption. Yogis may be interested to learn it is said to cleanse the channels, balance the chakras and support the ligaments.

Pregnant women need to exercise caution with turmeric supplements during pregnancy as it has been linked to miscarriage. Best to discuss this with your doctor if you are concerned.

GOOD FOR YOU	NOT SO GOOD FOR YOU
Fruits Favour sweet fruits. Apricots, avocado, coconut, dates, figs (fresh), grapes, lemons, limes, oranges, pineapple, plums, quince, raisins (soaked), rhubarb, soursop, strawberries, tamarind, tangerines *In moderation* Apples, bananas, berries (sweet), cherries, grapefruits, kiwifruit, mango, melons (sweet), papaya, peaches, pears, pomegranate	**Fruits** Dried fruits, cranberries, pears, persimmon, prunes, sour fruits in excess, watermelon
Vegetables Eat most cooked vegetables in season, cook with warming Vata favoured spices. Artichoke, asparagus, bok choy, beetroots, carrots, cucumber, daikon, fenugreek greens (methi), green beans, horseradish, leeks, mustard greens, okra, olives, onions, parsnip, pumpkin, squash (winter), sweet potato, zucchini *In moderation* Beetroot, broccoli, cabbage, cauliflower, capsicum, cucumber, endive, kale, lettuce, onion, peas, potato, radicchio, radish, spinach, sprouts, watercress	**Vegetables** Brussels sprouts, eggplant, mushrooms, shiitake mushrooms, onions (raw), Swiss chard, tomatoes, turnips
Grains Vatas should avoid having a diet based only on brown rice. Basmati rice (brown and white) *In moderation* Brown rice, long grain rice, quinoa, wild rice	**Grains** Buckwheat, corn, millet, dry puffed cereals, packet cereals with cold milk
Legumes Aduki beans, mung beans, tofu (cooked) *In moderation* Urad dhal	**Legumes** Black beans, chickpeas, kidney beans, brown and red lentils, soybeans, tempeh, lima beans, navy beans, pinto beans, split peas, white beans
Dairy Buttermilk, cottage cheese, cow's milk, ghee, yoghurt *In moderation* Cheeses (hard or soft), goat's milk, sour cream	**Dairy** Ice-cream
Animal foods Chicken (dark), duck and duck eggs, eggs, fish (all), prawns, turkey (dark) *In moderation* Beef	**Animal foods** Chicken (white), lamb, pork, rabbit, turkey (white), venison

GOOD FOR YOU	NOT SO GOOD FOR YOU
Sweeteners Brown rice syrup, brown sugar, fructose, juice concentrates, jaggery, maple syrup, sugar cane juice, palm sugar, raw sugar, dates *In moderation* Dried fruits, molasses, honey (if added as a flavour over foods to sweeten or added to warm drinks)	**Sweeteners** Honey (cooked), sugar substitutes, white sugar
Nuts and seeds Almonds, Brazil nuts, cashews, chestnuts, hazelnuts, macadamias, peanuts, pecans, pinenuts, pistachios, walnuts, pumpkin seeds, sesame seeds, sunflower seeds, coconut, chia, flaxseed (linseed) *In moderation* Peanuts	**Nuts and seeds** *In moderation* Psyllium
Herbs and spices Amchur (mango powder), anise, asafoetida (hing), basil, bayleaf, black pepper, caraway, cardamom, chilli pepper, cinnamon, cloves, coriander, cumin, curry powder, dill, fennel, garam masala, ginger (fresh and dried), kudzu, mace, mustard seeds, nutmeg, oregano, paprika, peppermint, pippali (long pepper), rosemary, rosewater, saffron, sage, savoury, spearmint, star anise, tamarind, tarragon, thyme, turmeric, vanilla *In moderation* Cayenne, coriander, curry leaves, fenugreek, garlic (cooked), horseradish, mint, parsley	**Herbs and spices** Curry leaves (neem), garlic (raw)
Teas Bancha, basil, chamomile, chicory, cinnamon, cloves, elderflower, fennel, ginger, lavender, licorice, orange peel, peppermint, rose, rosehip, saffron *In moderation* Chrysanthemum, ginger, hibiscus, jasmine	**Teas** Dandelion, corn silk
Beverages Almond milk, carob-flavoured milk, coconut milk, soy milk (spiced and hot); homemade lemonade; berry, carrot, grape, mango, orange, pineapple juices *In moderation* Milkshakes, mixed vegetable juices	**Beverages** Alcohol, caffeinated beverages, carbonated drinks, icy cold drinks, iced tea, soy milk (cold); apple, cranberry, pear, prune, tomato juices

PITTA

GOOD FOR YOU	NOT SO GOOD FOR YOU
Fruits Sweet fruits; apples, berries (sweet), avocado, coconut, figs, fresh goji berries, grapes (dark), mango, melons, oranges, pears, pineapples (sweet), plums, pomegranate, prunes, raisins, watermelon *In moderation** Avocado, dried sweet fruits, kiwifruit, lemons, limes, quince, strawberries, tamarind ** In moderation in their season so Vata in autumn/early winter and Kapha spring*	**Fruits** Bananas, berries (sour), cherries (sour), cranberries, grapes (green), grapefruit, papaya, peaches, persimmon, rhubarb, soursop
Vegetables Sweet and bitter vegetables; artichoke, asparagus, beetroot (cooked), bell pepper, broccoli, brussels sprouts, cabbage, cauliflower, carrots (cooked), celery, collard greens, coriander, corn, cucumber, daikon, dandelion greens, endive, green beans, Jerusalem artichoke, kale, kohlrabi, landcress, leafy greens, leeks, lettuce, mushroom, okra, parsnips, peas, potatoes (white), radicchio, rocket, sprouts, spinach (cooked and raw), spirulina, sweet potato, winter squash (acorn, butternut, spaghetti), watercress, zucchini *In moderation* Bamboo shoot, carrot, celery, corn, daikon, kohlrabi, leeks, mustard greens, parsley, pumpkin, spinach	**Vegetables** Beetroot (raw), eggplant, horseradish, hot chilli pepper, garlic, onion (raw), radish, Swiss chard, taro root, tomatoes, turnip
Grains Rice (basmati brown), rice (white) *In moderation* Sushi rice, brown rice, medium grain rice	**Grains** Buckwheat, corn, millet, quinoa, rice (all other rices not listed in Good for You column)
Legumes Aduki, black beans, black eyed peas, chickpeas, kidney beans, lentils (all but red), lima beans, mung dhal (whole or split), navy beans, pinto beans, soybeans, soy milk, cheese, split peas (green and yellow), tempeh, tofu, urid *In moderation* Tempeh, tofu cooked	**Legumes** Lentils (red), toor dhal
Dairy Butter (unsalted), cheese (fresh, soft not aged, unsalted), cottage cheese, cow's milk (unhomogenised), ghee, goat's milk, ice-cream (homemade), yoghurt (sweetened)	**Dairy** Butter (salted), buttermilk, cheese (hard), labneh, goat's cheese, feta, haloumi, parmesan, sour cream, yoghurt (frozen, fruit, plain with fruit)

GOOD FOR YOU	NOT SO GOOD FOR YOU
Sweeteners	**Sweeteners**
Brown sugar, unrefined, fruit juice concentrates, fructose, dates, honey, jaggery, maple syrup, rice syrup, raw sugar, succanat	Molasses, sugar substitutes, white sugar
In moderation	
Brown rice syrup, rice milk	
Meats	**Meats**
Chicken (white), eggs (white), fish (freshwater), rabbit, prawns, turkey (white), venison	Beef, chicken (dark), eggs (yolk), fish (sea), lamb, mutton, pork, turkey (dark)
Nuts and seeds	**Nuts and seeds**
Not too many nuts as they are heating	All nuts, sesame seeds, black and white, tahini
In moderation	
Almonds (soaked overnight and peeled), coconut, flaxseeds (linseed), sunflower seeds, pumpkin seeds, pysllium	
Herbs and spices	**Herbs and spices**
Cumin, coriander (fresh and dried), curry leaves, dill fresh, fennel, ginger (fresh), nutmeg, kudzu, mint, peppermint, parsley, saffron, turmeric	Ajwan, allspice, amchur (mango powder), anise, asafoetida (hing), bay leaf, cayenne, chilli powder, fenugreek, garlic, ginger (dry), marjoram, miso, mustard seeds, oregano, paprika, pippali (long pepper), rosemary, thyme, sage
In moderation	
Basil, black pepper, caraway, cardamom, cinnamon, cloves, curry powder, dill seeds, garam masala, ginger (fresh), mace, nutmeg, orange peel, parsley, tamarind, vanilla	
Teas	**Teas**
Alfalfa, bancha, blackberry, cardamom, cinnamon, chamomile, elderflower, fennel, ginger (fresh), hibiscus, jasmine, lavender, lemon balm, licorice, marshmallow, mint, raspberry leaf, rose flower, rosehip, saffron	Ajwan, clove, corn silk, eucalyptus, ginger (dried), ginseng, pennyroyal, sage, sassafras
In moderation	
Cardamom, cinnamon, rosehips, strawberry	
Beverages	**Beverages**
Alcohol (beer, dry white wine); aloe vera, apple, apricot, berry, grape, mango, orange, peach, pear, pomegranate, prune juices; coconut milk, coconut water, cow's milk, dandelion, rice milk, soy milk	Alcohol (hard spirits, red wine), caffeinated beverages, chocolate milk, cranberry juice, grapefruit juice, icy cold drinks, iced tea, lemonade, pineapple juice, tomato juice
In moderation	
Almond milk, carrot vegetable juice, chicory blends, orange juice, lassi, soy milk (spiced)	

GOOD FOR YOU	NOT SO GOOD FOR YOU
Fruits Apples, apricots, berries, cherries, dried fruit, figs (dried), peaches, pears, persimmon, pomegranate, quince, raisins *In moderation* Grapes, kiwifruit, lemons, limes, mango, oranges, strawberries, tangerine, tamarind	**Fruits** Excessively sweet, sour or watery fruits; avocado, banana, coconut, cranberries, dates, figs (fresh), grapefruit, melons, papaya, pineapple, plums, rhubarb, soursop, watermelon
Vegetables Pungent bitter vegetables; asparagus, beetroot and greens, bok choy, broccoli, brussels sprouts, cabbage, capsicum, carrots, cauliflower, celery, chilli, corn, daikon, eggplant, endive, green beans, kale, leeks, lettuce, leafy greens, okra, onions, peas, peppers, potato (white), sprouts, rockets, spinach, sprouts, squash (winter), turnips, tomato (cooked), watercress *In moderation* Artichoke	**Vegetables** Sweet and juicy vegetables; cucumber, mushrooms, olives, (black or green), parsnips, potato (sweet), pumpkin, squash (summer), tomato (raw)
Grains Buckwheat, quinoa, corn, millet *In moderation* Basmati rice, amaranth, quinoa	**Grains** Brown rice, rice flour
Legumes Aduki, black beans, chickpeas, lentils (all), navy beans, peas (dried), pinto beans, soy milk, tempeh, tofu (hot) *In moderation* Mung beans (moong dhal)	**Legumes** Kidney beans, miso, soy beans, soy cheese, tamari, tofu (cold)
Meats Chicken (white), eggs (not fried), fish (freshwater), rabbit, shrimp, turkey (white)	**Meats** Beef, chicken (dark), fish (sea), lamb, mutton, pork

GOOD FOR YOU	NOT SO GOOD FOR YOU
Dairy Kapha should use dairy with moderation. *In moderation* Ghee, goat's cheese (unsalted and not aged), goat's milk	**Dairy** Butter, cheese (most), cow's milk, ice-cream, sour cream, yoghurt (plain, with fruit, or frozen)
Sweeteners Raw honey *In moderation* Brown rice syrup, dates, maple, fruit juice, dried fruits	**Sweeteners** Fructose, brown sugar, molasses, natural sugar, sugar substitutes, white sugar
Nuts and seeds *In moderation* Flaxseeds (linseeds), pumpkin, sunflower, coconut, sesame seeds	**Nuts and seeds** All nuts
Herbs and spices All spices are good. *In moderation* Fennel, fenugreek, ginger (fresh), mint, tamarind, vanilla	**Herbs and spices**
Teas Bancha, basil, black tea (well spiced), chamomile, chicory, cinnamon, clove, dandelion, ginger (dried), jasmine, lavender, orange peel, peppermint, raspberry, saffron	**Teas** Fennel, ginger (fresh), ginseng, licorice, marshmallow, rosehip
Beverages Kapha should drink fruit juices in moderation. Too much dairy, alcohol or caffeinated drinks will all have a negative impact on Kapha types. All fruit juices should be diluted. *In moderation* Apple, apricot, berry, carrot, cherry, cranberry, mixed vegetable, pear, pineapple, pomegranate, prune juices; soy milk; alcohol, almond milk, caffeinated drinks	**Beverages** Banana smoothies, carbonated drinks, chocolate drinks, coconut milk, lemonade, orange juice, tomato juice, grapefruit juice, salted and sour drinks; chilled drinks

The six best doctors: sunshine, water, rest, air, exercise and diet.

–Buddha

Big, big heartfelt thank yous to:

My Higher Power. Living a spiritual life one day at time is bloody scary for a Pitta control freak. You lighten my load and continue to create life changing miracles when I'm brave enough to let you. My publisher, Jo Mackay. I am so happy we can now speak Ayurveda to each other. Thank you for wanting to understand the magic of Ayurveda and for encouraging me to write more than recipes this time around. Luisa Brimble, photographer, for your stunning images and your effervescent approach to work. Theressa Klein, photo chef, you made every dish look incredible. You excel at what you do and I feel honoured to have your kindness and friendship in my life. Emmaly Stewart, props stylist, your ability to choose a minimal amount of stunning pieces to give this girl her special look and feel was truly impressive. Food editor, Megan Johnston, who is just so damn easy to work with it is a joy. Deborah Nixon, my words editor, who got the upfront text in shape. Julia Knapman for tidying up the words at proof stage. Kristen Ingemar, who tested all of the recipes alongside me, I'm always grateful for your positive and well considered feedback and criticism. Miranda O'Rourke and Harrison Balodis, my children/not really my children but the closest thing I'm ever going to have to them. So special to have your beautiful faces on these pages. Thank you both for helping me find my home in the green rolling hills. I love you to bits. My dear super sandwich maker Yvonne who ensured I was OK to go when I was totally traumatised by a 5-day-late removalist. My darling sister Paulie and nephew Beau who came and ensured my garden was in shipshape order for photography. My family who continue to encourage and love me and my patient and supportive friends who continue to share my enthusiasm for yet another cookbook. Dear Tracey Findlay who encouraged and listened to me whenever I lost my bundle about this book. I feel so fortunate to know you and have your friendship and guidance. My new Tilba friends, for welcoming me into your lives, your community and your big open generous hearts. Darling Cliffy boy. You are my gold and diamonds, little man. I love that you happily eat dhal, kitchari and congee with me. That you continue to chase the chooks, sheep and cows even when you know you are not meant to. But most of all I love that you are at peace by my side wherever I am, just hanging out, you and I living our simple life and loving it as much as we possibly can. When I stumble and sometimes fall I love that you lick the tears from my cheek, then lay your head on my chest and assure me you've got it covered until I'm ready to get back up again. My wise and learned Ayurvedic teachers whose courses, workshops, books, websites, podcasts and ongoing commitment to sharing Ayurveda with the world allow me to continue learning about this life-enriching tradition from wherever I am in the world. I feel such deep gratitude to Dr Ajit, Dr Claudia Welch, Dr Robert Svoboda, Dr Vasant Lad, Cate Stillman, Maya Tiwari, Dr John Douillard and Deepak Chopra. Also to Jennifer Barnes and Louise Maudlin, my cherished Ayurvedic sisterhood who never mind me running my Ayurvedic questions by them. Special thank you to darling Jen for your help with the daily routine section of the book and for sharing your chai secrets with me.

And to you for purchasing this love-filled book. I truly hope you welcome her into your kitchen, and may her recipes nourish you in the way they were intended to. May your life be happy, may you be healthy, may you be peaceful, may you live with ease.

Namaste

X Jody

We shot this book on my new little farm in Tilba. I feel so happy inside to be sharing a snapshot of my new life with you.

Index

HQ
An imprint of HarperCollinsPublishers Ltd
1 London Bridge Street
London SE1 9GF

First published by HQ Non Fiction, an imprint of Harlequin Enterprises (Australia) Pty Limited
Published in Great Britain by HQ
An imprint of HarperCollinsPublishers Ltd 2019

ISBN 978-0-00-797732-1

Printed and bound in China by C & C Offset Printing Company Ltd